THE ASTONISHING TRUTH
ABOUT THE WORLD'S GREATEST FOOD

Heather!
Cacao = Love!

NAKED
chocolate

DAVID WOLFE AND SHAZZIE

Ca·cao. Pronounced [ka-kow]. Rhymes with "cow."

E·lix·ir : An aromatic solution serving as a vehicle for medicine... A substance believed to maintain life indefinitely. Also called elixir of life... A substance of transmutative properties... Alchemy: An imaginary liquor capable of transmuting metals into gold; also, one for producing life indefinitely; as, elixir vit[ae], or the elixir of life... The refined spirit; the quintessence... Any cordial or substance which invigorates... A substance believed to cure all ills... The philosopher's stone.

WWW.NAKED-CHOCOLATE.COM

North Atlantic Books
Berkeley, California

Copyright

Published by

North Atlantic Books
P.O. Box 12327
Berkeley, California 94712

ISBN 978-1-55643-731-1

Book design, art, and layout by Shazzie
(with assistance from David Wolfe)
Cover art by Amy Gayheart

Printed in the United States of America

Naked Chocolate is sponsored by the Society for the Study of Native Arts and Sciences, a nonprofit educational corporation whose goals are to develop an educational and cross-cultural perspective linking various scientific, social, and artistic fields; to nurture a holistic view of arts, sciences, humanities, and healing; and to publish and distribute literature on the relationship of mind, body, and nature.

North Atlantic Books' publications are available through most bookstores. For further information, visit www.northatlanticbooks.com or call 800-733-3000.

Disclaimer

This book is sold for information purposes only. Neither the authors nor the publisher will be held accountable for the use or misuse of the information contained in this book. This book is not intended as medical advice, because the authors and publisher of this work are not medical doctors and do not recommend the use of medicines to achieve the best day ever or to alleviate health challenges. Because there is always some risk involved, the authors, publisher, and/or distributors of this book are not responsible for any adverse effects or consequences resulting from the use of any recipes, suggestions or procedures described hereafter.

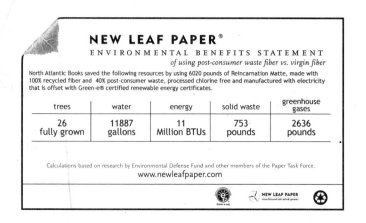

NEW LEAF PAPER®

ENVIRONMENTAL BENEFITS STATEMENT

of using post-consumer waste fiber vs. virgin fiber

North Atlantic Books saved the following resources by using 6020 pounds of Reincarnation Matte, made with 100% recycled fiber and 40% post-consumer waste, processed chlorine free and manufactured with electricity that is offset with Green-e® certified renewable energy certificates.

trees	water	energy	solid waste	greenhouse gases
26 fully grown	11887 gallons	11 Million BTUs	753 pounds	2636 pounds

Calculations based on research by Environmental Defense Fund and other members of the Paper Task Force.
www.newleafpaper.com

NEW LEAF PAPER
manufactured with wind power

2 3 4 5 6 7 8 UNITED 15 14 13 12 11

A Note to the Reader

Each lesson in this book contains facts, concepts, and ideas which build upon the chapter before it. Therefore, on the first time through, we urge the reader to avoid skipping the earlier chapters. The reading will surely prove most fruitful if you begin at the Table of Contents and read straight through.

Naked Chocolate is written in British English, not American English. Both authors prefer the British spellings.

Many of the products mentioned in this book are available from Longevity Warehouse in the USA and Canada (www.longevitywarehouse.com) and Rawcreation Ltd in the UK (www.detoxyourworld.com). Longevity Warehouse and Rawcreation Ltd are committed to providing the most incredible and unique health and beauty products available in the world today. All products are diligently researched and tested before they are chosen for distribution.

A Note on References

Due to the haphazard chaos magic research process that created this book, some references to studies and facts were lost. If you find information in this book that is unreferenced or unsubstantiated with a reference, we recommend that you do the book and Internet research to corroborate the information. If you find a reference that we neglected to credit, please e-mail it to us via Facebook at www.facebook.com/doxtor or www.facebook.com/DavidAvocadoWolfe so that we may include it in future editions of this book.

A Mayan ball player giving a cacao fruit to a deity

Acknowledgments from David

Amy Gayheart — Thank you for the flyers, labels, smiles, great times and high vibes! A huge thank you from us both for your stunning cover design.

Anita Arze — For all the chocolate-loving good times!

Camille "Super Goji Girl" Perrin Giglio — You are a chocolate super-hero.

The Coconut Brothers — Ethan and Eli Schotz for bringing into our awareness the true meaning and importance of raw cacao beans.

Sky Dancer — For all the best times ever and for supplying us with raw chocolate from Palenque during our European Tour in the summer of 2003.

Acknowledgments from Shazzie

Matt — Bless you for helping me maintain focus when creating this book, while I was also growing our Evie and sometimes feeling quite sick of chocolate, along with everything else!

Toby Darling — Your testing tastebuds were most welcomed.

Peppermint Pattie — For helping me create some of the recipes when I couldn't tell you why because this book was still a secret then!

The Coconut Brothers — Ethan and Eli — you are the cutest chocolate givers in the whole world! Now look what you started!

Mum and Jennie (at www.detoxyourworld.com) — Thank you for being part of my love-empire — I'm so glad you're growing with me! And thank you for being my family, along with my lovely Dad!

Table of Contents

Introduction

"Forget love—
I'd rather fall in chocolate!"
— Anonymous

There is nothing in the world like chocolate. It is luxurious, sensuous, delightful, passionate, inspirational, sexual and exciting to all senses.

According to popular research, chocolate is the number one food craved by women. Chocolate's unique chemistry, taste and sensory properties make it one of the most popular food substances in the United States and Western culture in general. Americans consume, on average, 11.7 pounds (5.3 kilograms) of chocolate per person annually.

Whatever mystery is behind it, there is no end in sight for the exploding chocolate renaissance. The world-wide consumption of chocolate is increasing at a rate of 3 to 4% each year! Switzerland leads the world in chocolate consumption at 19 pounds per person per year. The Norwegians and British are tied for second, with an average consumption of 17.5 pounds of chocolate annually. Behind them are the Belgians, Dutch, Germans, and Austrians, who eat more than 14 pounds each year. The annual intake of chocolate in Japan is only 3 pounds.

Western culture has fallen in love with this most amazing substance. Yet, for most of us, it has been a blind date all along. After all, what is chocolate? Where does it come from?

This book is about bringing the sacred spirit back into chocolate, the raw spirit from whence it originates, the pure energy of cacao, "the food of the gods." All chocolate is made from cacao, the seed of the fruit of a jungle tree!

Throughout most of our lives it was a general mystery to us where chocolate came from. There always seemed to be a cloud around the whole process. Now it is time to dispel the ambiguity surrounding chocolate once and for all and lay naked before the world the true meaning of chocolate. That is our purpose and mission.

David

Sometime, when we were kids, probably at my Aunt Dee-Dee's house in Moberly, Missouri, I first viewed the film *Willie Wonka and the Chocolate Factory*. That was my first exposure to the deep, mystical magic of chocolate. Sometime shortly thereafter, my family drove to Hershey, Pennsylvania to experience the Hershey's Chocolate Theme Park. It was then I realised that chocolate had something more to offer than your average burger and fries.

A casual interest in chocolate throughout my life has blossomed into a passion and incredible fascination for the cacao tree and its prodigal product, the cacao bean. Cacao beans are the raw form of chocolate. They are the key ingredient of all chocolate. All chocolate is made from cacao beans.

For many years, whenever I would come across raw cacao beans in Hawaii, I would peel a few of them and throw them into a smoothie or coconut drink. I never experimented with them enough to realise what I was dealing with.

One day Shazzie and I were visiting our friends Ethan and Eli in Maui. We were peeling cacao beans for a smoothie and Eli asked me, "Have you ever just eaten one?" And the truth was, I hadn't. So I peeled one and just as I bit into it a tremendous download of information hit me. It was a life-changing experience. I was surprised to discover how incredible it is to eat raw cacao beans by themselves — to eat **Naked Chocolate**.

Subsequent research and experience has clearly demonstrated to Shazzie and I that the raw cacao bean is nature's most fantastic superfood. Nature has already fashioned the most fantastic medicine! There is extraordinary hope for chocoholics everywhere! You can turn guilt, addictions and misconceptions into super-nutrition and the best day ever!

Eli and David in Maui

Shazzie

As a child, chocolate for me was often a no-go area. I loved the stuff (who doesn't?), but it left me with terrible migraines. I had to ration my chocolate, and was probably the only child in England to have some Easter egg left on the Monday! This obviously brought me several fair-weathered friends. And cousins. And parents.

Shazzie in Maui with her first live organic chocolate drink

I've always loved experimenting with foods, and my favourite meal at one time was Kit Kat and cheese toasted sandwiches. I'd love opening up the bread and seeing all the melted mess, and I'd joke that it looked like the Elephant Man. I was a sick child.

When I grew up, and grew out of migraines, I began to love bitter foods, and spent years devouring espresso coffee with dark 70% chocolate dipped into it. Another favourite meal was chocolate and crisps together. And of course there were chocolate ice creams, hot chocolate, pan au chocolat, chocolate mousse, chocolate cake and everything else brown and melty-in-the-mouth. Even as a long-term vegan, I could satisfy my love for chocolate.

Then I became a raw foodist and it all changed. Raw fooders can't eat chocolate bars because all processed chocolate is cooked! In a slightly bereft state, chocolate didn't pass my lips for over three years. Then came that wonderful, ground-breaking fateful day in Maui that David describes. As we were gorging on these beans, he said to me "I've never seen you go for any food in the way you've gone for this". And it was true! I was lighting up, I was oblivious to everything else going on, and I was so happy to be reunited with my old love.

A few months later in Amsterdam, David and I were having massive chocolate experiences whilst reading **Charlie and the Chocolate Factory**. We started to write, share ideas and form the beginnings of **Naked Chocolate**. It was hilarious — walking around this mad city, seeing everything through switched-on chocolate eyes!

And now the book is complete, my love for chocolate has blossomed into an everlasting relationship, never again to be lost, yet forever changed.

Cacao's Properties

The key to chocolate's super qualities seems to be eating it in its raw, natural state as a cacao bean! When cacao beans are excessively heated, melted, processed, chemicalised and added to dairy products, they lose key nutrient qualities of texture, psychoactive properties, brain nutrition and more. Other properties of the cacao bean are still present yet diminished by cooking, such as dark chocolate flavours, antioxidants, aphrodisiac qualities, mood elevation and others. Yet certain properties of chocolate appear due to cooking which are unfavourable, such as becoming allergic or having intense cravings or addictions.

Consider that in present-day chocolate manufacturing, large machines are heating the cacao beans anywhere from 248 to 266 degrees Fahrenheit (120 to 130 degrees Celsius). After roasting, the beans are cooled off and then flowed through rollers where they are cracked so as to separate the skins from the beans. Air blowers blow over the assembly line blowing the skins away from the roasted cacao. These roasted cacaos without their skins are called cacao nibs. The cacao nibs are then ground. The intense heat of the grinding liquifies the cacao oils which turns the cacao nibs into *chocolate liquor*. This is allowed to cool. During the next phase of manufacturing, the *chocolate liquor* is sent into a mechanical press. The cacao oil/butter (known to most as cocoa butter) is pressed out of the liquor, filtered and collected separately. The remaining cacao solids are pressed into cakes. The cacao cakes are then made into cacao powder (cocoa powder). Potassium carbonate is added to the powder as an alkalising agent (to raise pH) so that the powder is soluble in water, otherwise the powder will clump together in water. Even something as simple sounding as cocoa powder is a lot more complex than one might imagine!

Chocolatiers at that point begin to work their alchemy of bringing in various ingredients to create chocolate treats. Of course when we are dealing with large-scale mass-production, various insect and rodent contaminants may have already made their way into the chocolate manufacturing.

Conching is an additional mixing and blending step that chocolatiers use to knead their chocolate mixtures together. This manufacturing step is called conching because the original machines were shaped like a conch shell. Once the mixture has been conched, it is usually tempered (or reheated to 150 degrees Fahrenheit or 66 degrees Celsius), then cooled into molds and shapes. This keeps the cacao butter from crystallising and affecting the appearance of the chocolate.

The typical commercial chocolate sample will contain a mixture of the alkalised cacao powder, cacao butter, genetically-modified soy lecithin, vanilla extract and refined sugar. Milk chocolate contains powdered milk with its harmful antioxidant-blocking properties and a vast array of pesticide residues and artificial hormone residues that have been fed to the animal.

After all this, no wonder people want the real thing. What happened to the original food, the cacao bean?

We as a culture, as a species, had gone so far into eating anything and everything without any thought of the consequences or the dangers that we are now realising that we had loaded ourselves with all sorts of artificial chemicals, additives, pesticides, colourings, carcinogens, etc. Now, a new consciousness is among us, one that seeks to get back to the source, to find the real food behind what has been processed beyond all reason.

After centuries of industrial age food, people are fed up. We are now seeing a return to the magic of pure food — simplicity, originality and food made with love. Let us get back to the real food beneath all the layers of cooking, machining, pressing, conching and tempering. Let us have food without insect parts, chemical additives, bovine growth hormone, pesticides or rat pieces! Let us have the actual food, the exotic food, the food made with love that is unadulterated so that we may know the truth!

We do not live in the industrial age anymore. We live in the information age where anything is possible. The Internet helps this happen. We can have the best food ever if we choose! We can have the best chocolate ever if we choose! We can have real, raw, organic cacao beans grown with love shipped to our door, if that is our choice!

We invite you to discover an entirely new raw experience: Naked Chocolate. It is our contention that chocolate was never meant to be adulterated.

We have always held out hope that we could live forever on desserts! And now we find out that all the desserts can be chocolate-covered! Outrageous! Flip your stress around by living on desserts (after all, "desserts" spelled backwards is "stressed!").

With love, **David Wolfe** and **Shazzie**

Part I: Cacao

"The beverage of the gods was Ambrosia; that of man is chocolate. Both increase the length of life in a prodigious manner."
— Louis Lewin, MD,
Phantastica

Legends of Cacao

Central America (Mayan)

The chief Mayan deity, *Heart of Sky*, after he had created the world, the trees, the grasses, all the creatures in the sea, the birds and animals on the land, had one thing left to do, and that was to create humanity. *Heart of Sky* made attempts using mud, then wood, then stone; however, they were all unsuccessful. Eventually, using ingenuity and creativity, *Heart of Sky* fashioned a human being out of materials from nature: water, earth, wood, corn, many fruits and cacao. And so humans came into being with cacao being one of the essential ingredients.

Central America (Quetzalcoatl)

In one myth, it was *Quetzalcoatl*, the plumed serpent, who first brought cacao beans from the Garden of Life to Earth. *Quetzalcoatl*, with his plumed serpent imagery, was one of the most revered and respected deities in the mythology of ancient Central America. He taught people the art of agriculture, medicine and cacao growing. He did not like human sacrifice and was well loved by the people.

South America (Peru)

Khuno, the god of storms, destroyed a village with torrential rain and hail because he was angry at the people for having set fire to the jungle to clear land for their crops. After the storm, the people found a cacao tree. This, they say, is how cacao came into cultivation. Cacao showed these people how to live in harmony with the jungle.

South America

A myth from the northern Andes describes the crucial role played by cacao in restoring the balance of nature after a greedy deity snatched all the wealth for himself.

The myth begins with an omnipotent deity named *Sibu* who could grow animals and humans from seeds. *Sibu* transferred his powers to another deity, *Sura*, giving him all the precious seeds. One day, *Sura* buried the seeds and left the site for a few moments. Unfortunately, while he was away, a third deity, the trickster *Jabaru* dug up all the seeds and ate them, leaving nothing for the creation-work of *Sibu* and *Sura*. When *Sura* returned, the trickster *Jabaru* slit *Sura's* throat and buried him where the seeds had been. Very pleased with himself, *Jabaru* left the scene and went home to his wives.

After some time, the trickster *Jabaru* passed by the place again and saw that two strange trees had sprung up from *Sura's* grave: a cacao tree and a calabash. The deity *Sibu* was there too, and he stood quietly beside the trees. When *Sibu* saw the trickster approaching, he asked him to make a cacao drink from the tree. The trickster picked a bean-filled cacao pod and a calabash fruit and took them to his wives, who brewed the cacao and filled the hollowed out calabash shell with the rich drink. Then the trickster carried the cacao drink back to *Sibu*, holding it out to him. "No, you drink first," *Sibu* insisted politely. *Jabaru* complied eagerly, gulping down the delicious drink as fast as he could. But his delight changed to agony as the cacao born from poor *Sura's* body caused *Jabaru's* belly to swell and swell until it burst wide open, spilling out the stolen seeds all over the ground.

Sibu then restored his friend *Sura* to life again and returned the seeds to him so that all humans and animals might one day grow from those precious seeds and enjoy Earth's bounty.

The mythology of cacao has great bearing on the current state of the world. The upsurgence of the desire for cacao is the myth playing itself out eternally. The general theme of the legends describes that when humanity begins to misappropriate nature by cutting down jungles and misusing natural resources, then the cacao tree, its fruit and seeds are introduced to restore harmony with nature. City-based cultures, like the trickster *Jabaru*, are greedily swallowing the seeds of life for future generations of plants, animals and humans. Essentially, when the balance between humanity and nature is lost, then cacao arrives to save the day.

Theobroma Cacao (The Chocolate Tree)

"Within this pucaminious husk or large fruit, is the *Cacahuatl* or (as the Spaniards corruptly call them) the Cacao nuts, being about the bigness of Almonds, each of them enveloped in a slimy substance, and film, of Plegmatique complexion, but of a most refreshing taste: which women love to suck of from the Cacao, finding it cool, and in the mouth dissolving into water." — Dr Henry Stubbe, **The Indian Nectar** (1662)

In 1753 Carl von Linnaeus, the Swedish scientist, thought that chocolate was so important that he named the genus and species of the chocolate tree himself. He named this tree *Theobroma cacao*, which literally means: cacao, the food of the gods. Just what the indigenous native Central Americans called it.

Cultivated *Theobroma cacao* trees typically grow anywhere from 10 to 30 feet (3 to 10 meters) in height. The tree begins branching fairly close to the Earth and from its branches spring the dark green, avocado-tree-like leaves of the cacao tree. The leaves are anywhere from 10-25 centimetres in length and about 5-8 centimeters wide.

Theobroma cacao with fruit

The cacao tree flowers and produces fruit all year long. The cauliflori flowers are five-petalled, pale, lightly-scented mushroom-like growths that grow straight out of the trunk or large branches.

Cacao flowers are best pollinated by tiny insects called midges. At least six different types of midges are known to help pollinate cacao.

Once pollinated, each flower develops into a pod-fruit. The fruits typically begin as green in colour and develop into characteristic red, orange, yellow, blue or purple varieties. It takes five or six months for each fruit pod to ripen. The fruits usually grow to 18-20 centimetres in length. Each fruit contains anywhere from 20 to 50 almond-like seeds or "beans" surrounded by a sweet, thin pulp. It is these seeds that we call "the food of the gods" or cacao beans — the raw, natural form of chocolate.

For point of reference, the seeds of each fruit are enough to make about three to four high-quality dark chocolate bars.

The cacao fruit is hard-shelled and does not fall to the jungle floor when ripe. In the wild, the ripe cacao fruits are gnawed into by monkeys, birds (macaws, parrots, etc.), bats and other jungle animals. Typically, some of the seeds fall in the jungle forest and, with good conditions, a new tree is born.

Cacao seeds actually sprout quite easily. And young trees can bear fruit within three to five years in a proper growing environment. Historically, fresh cacao seeds were planted in accordance with the phases of the moon.

A mature cacao tree will produce about 50 fruits, usually harvested twice a year. Cacao trees bear fruits all year long. Like coconuts, there is no true season.

The cacao tree likes well drained soils with a high content of organic matter. As long as it has that type of soil, close companion trees do not bother it. Such trees and plants as annona trees (cherimoya family), avocado trees, bananas, coconut palms, legume-shade trees, oil palms, rubber trees, and many other tropicals are intercropped with cacao. Typically, on cacao plantations, the cacao trees may be spaced as close as 3 meters from each other.

Cacao trees grow best in the shade of larger trees where they are protected from wind and excessive sun. Peter Martyr D'Angheira, in **De Orbo Novo** (1530) noted: "They are planted under the shade of a tree which protects them from the sun's rays or against the dangers of fog, just as a child is sheltered in the bosom of a nurse."

Cacao trees like to grow inside the latitudes of 20 degrees north and 20 degrees south of the Equator. Within this zone, cacao trees can adapt to a large range of tropical conditions (from extremely humid to drier regions), but they must have warm temperatures to thrive (79 degrees Fahrenheit or 21 degrees Celsius is ideal). They like environments or altitudes where temperatures are above 60 degrees F (16 degrees C). They thrive best with minimal fluctuations of maintained high humidity.

Indigenous to Central and South America and probably originating in the Orinoco river basin in Venezuela, cacao trees have since been spread to most tropical climates in the 20 degree latitude zone and now grow all over the world.

Bioko, a small island near the equator off the coast of west Africa, was the first site of cacao cultivation outside of the Americas. Farmers planted cacao from Venezuela there in 1590. This island with its well-drained soil, tropical rain patterns and warm climate possesses a perfect climate for cacao. Bioko became the launch-point for cacao into Africa. The island is now part of the African nation of Guinea. Today, farmers there produce 8,000 tons of cacao beans each year accounting for 70 percent of the nation's export wealth.

Three or Ten Varieties of Cacao?

Three traditional species variations of *Theobroma cacao* are currently in wide cultivation around the world: *Criollo, Forastero,* and *Trinitario* (a cross of the other two).

Criollo (in Spanish means native-born), of the subspecies *Theobroma cacao,* originates from the mountainous tropics of Central America. It was the first cacao variety to be cultivated in pre-Columbian Central America. *Criollo* pods are elongated and deeply ridged, and are usually red or yellow. The *Criollo's* distinctive features include its exquisite flavour, its rich, varied taste and its full aroma. *Criollos* are dainty and delicate mountain cacaos that are often susceptible to disease, ripen late and have a relatively low yield and short productive fruiting life compared to other varieties. *Criollo* represents about 5 percent of the world crop and is under large-scale farming and domestication mainly (though not exclusively) in Venezuela, Ecuador, Colombia and Indonesia. In 1891, the Walter Baker Company in Massachusetts accurately characterised the *Criollo* variety. They wrote that it "is considered superior in size, colour, sweetness and oleaginous properties." *Criollo* is normally used in very fine chocolates, and has the most unique flavours, which can be floral, fruity, or spicy.

Forastero, of the subspecies *Theobroma cacao sphaerocarpum,* is also known as *Forastero amazonico* or *Amelonado.* Domesticated later than *Criollo,* the *Forastero's* wild ancestors proliferated in the Amazon basin. *Forastero* cacaos tend to be vigorous, robust plants that mature quickly and produce a rough chocolate. The pods vary in colour from yellowish to deep orange and are rounder than the *Criollo,* with less noticeable ridges (hence the name, *Amelonado,* "melon-shaped"). Because it is vigorous and disease-resistant, the *Forastero* accounts for most of the world's production (over 80 percent) and is grown mainly in Africa and Asia. *Forastero* beans can have over 50 percent fat content, and are commonly used to produce cocoa butter. *Forastero* is an easy-to-grow "work-horse" cacao variety that is generally considered adequate in flavour, yet certain cultivars can nevertheless have extraordinary flavour.

Trinitario is a hybrid of the *Criollo* and *Forastero* subspecies that dates back to the late eighteenth century. After a natural disaster that destroyed virtually all the *Criollo* on the island of Trinidad, *Forastero* trees were imported and the few surviving *Criollo* trees began to breed with the new ones to create the *Trinitario* variety. *Trinitario* possesses the delicate flavour, and aromatic properties of the *Criollo* and the hardiness of the *Forastero* plant. Today, *Trinitario* trees are grown mainly in Indonesia, Sri Lanka, South America and the West Indies. This variety accounts for about 10-15 percent of the world's cacao production and its beans have an average fat content of 56-58 percent.

Recent research indicates that the traditional three species variations of cacao should be updated to ten species variations. The suggested new categories and their geographical origins include: Amelonado — Brazil; Contamana — Peru; Criollo — Central America, Venezuela and Colombia; Curaray — Ecuador; Guiana — Guyane; Iquitos — Peru; Marañon — Brazil (Amazon) and Peru; Nacional — Ecuador; Nanay — Peru; Purús — Peru.

Cacao, Cocoa, Coco, Kola, Chocolate

The word "cacao" is extremely ancient and probably originated with the pre-Mayan Olmec peoples. Scholars David Stuart and Stephen D. Houston deciphered the word "ka-ka-wa" on a Mayan chocolate drinking vessel dating back thousands of years.

According to Allen M. Young's research in his book **The Chocolate Tree**, the Aztecs called the chocolate tree *cacvaqualhitl,* the fruit pods *cachooatl,* and prized cacao drink *chocolatl.*

Throughout this book, we typically use the terms cacao and chocolate interchangeably. There is confusion about the origin of the word "chocolate." The official dictionaries indicate that the word "chocolate" is derived from Nahuatl (the Aztec language) word chocolatl as Allen Young indicates. Michael Coe, Professor of Anthropology at Yale, and co-author of **The True History of Chocolate**, does not believe that *chocolatl* was actually an ancient Nahuatl word. He believes in the ideas of Mexican philologist Ignacio Davila Garibi who proposed that the

Mayan chocolate drinking vessel

"Spaniards had coined the new word by taking the Maya word chocol and then replacing the Maya word for "water," haa, with the Aztec one, atl." Another possibility is that "chocolate" is derived from the Mayan verb *chokola'j,* which means, "to drink chocolate together."

"Cocoa" is a British slang term for cacao. The actual present-day meaning of the word "cocoa" is the defatted, alkalised powder invented by the Dutchman Coenraad Van Houten in 1828.

The confusion about cacao becomes complicated, because we often hear "coco butter or coco" in regards to cacao. Cocoa butter or cocoa oil is the oil from the cacao bean. Coco butter, coco oil or coco, however, is associated with the coconut and its derivative products (coconut butter, coconut oil) and is a wonderful, though different entity entirely from *Theobroma cacao*.

Adding even more to the confusion is the word "coca" which is not related to cacao, but is in fact a leafy psychoactive stimulant shrub from the Andes which can be made into cocaine. Again, this is something different from *Theobroma cacao*.

If all of that was not enough, cacao should not be confused with its relative the African kola nut, which bestowed its name and caffeine, on the well-known soft drink.

A Brief History of Chocolate

According to the Linnaean categorisation system, the cacao tree is classified in the Sterculiaceae family (which also includes the African kola nut). And, more specifically, is a member of the neotropical Theobroma genus which contains at least 22 species.

In the Theobroma genus, there are other edible species similar to *Theobroma cacao* from which the chocolate bean or cacao bean is derived.

Theobroma bicolor is a well-cultivated related fruit tree grown primarily in Nicaragua for its fruity pulp which is pressed into a drink called *pinolillo* in Spanish or, in the Nahuatl language, is called *pataxte*. Another relative, *Theobroma augustifolia*, produces *cushta*, another food favourite in the Nicaraguan region.

Another loved variety, *Theobroma grandiflora*, produces the wonderful *capuacu* fruit. From this tree's branches covered with rust-shaded leaves grow clusters of exotic flowers that develop into brown, fuzzy, ovoid fruits that begin forming in the tree's eighth year. These fruits weigh between one and two kilograms and possess a pungent smell. The white pulp surrounding the cacao-like seeds is often used to create ice cream. This fruit tree grows in the humid Brazilian Amazon, but also enjoys the drier coastal state of Espirito Santo in Brazil.

Of course the most popular member of the Theobroma genus is cacao. According to the botanist Jose Cuatrecasas, there was an early, wide-spread territory for *Theobroma cacao* throughout the north and western portion of the Amazon river basin as well as in Central America and Southern Mexico. Various populations of this once wide-spread area were possibly cut off from each other over time in various ecological niches.

Other botanists believe that cacao is a wild South American tree brought forth into Central America by ancient Native American sea traders from the Orinoco river region or the Maracaibo basin of Venezuela or perhaps the upper Amazon.

Still others believe that *Theobroma cacao* was created by human cultivation as long as ten to fifteen thousand years ago by crossing two wild strains: *Theobroma pentagona* and *Theobroma leiocarpa*.

In any case, the origin of *Theobroma cacao* is still as mysterious as the magical chemistry contained within its fruit and seed.

Did you know that the cacao bean is the most revered of all rainforest foods? Cacao is the most pharmacologically complex food source in the known Amazon jungle, containing an estimated 1,200 individual chemical constituents (according to Joel Brenner's research in her book **The Emperors of Chocolate**)! This complexity is why chocolate cannot be synthesized artificially.

Human use of the cacao fruit and its seeds may be anywhere from 5,000 to 15,000 years old. The earliest known archeological evidence of cacao use was in a village in present-day Honduras, where pottery evidence of cacao use dates back to 2,000 BCE.

Olmec head

The first civilisation that we can guess had cultivated cacao is the Olmecs. The Olmecs lived in the area of Mexico we currently know as Veracruz and Tabasco. The Olmecs are known to history for the giant carved heads and the word "cacao" which they left behind.

The cacao tree seems to have had an affinity with the Olmec, African-featured peoples who inhabited the area of Central America, later inherited by the Mayans. Even today, the tree still has an affinity for brown-skinned, African Americans who often cultivate and harvest it in Central America and Northern South America, suggesting a deep spiritual connection between these peoples and this food. In recent history, *Theobroma cacao* seedlings were exported to Africa, which currently produces most of the world's cacao — one million tons per year!

The Mayans inherited their basic cacao knowledge from the Olmec peoples and made it a central part of their civilization. The last three rulers of the Mayan city of Tikal in present-day Guatemala were called Lord Cacao. A cacao tree is found carved on the Temple of the Wall Panels at Chichen Itza in the Yucatan. Cacao-shaped and cacao-depicting pottery items are found all over the Mayan areas of Central America.

The Mayans used cacao shamanistically and ritualistically. When the Spanish arrived in Central America, they were astonished to find that the "heathen" Maya had a baptism ritual for girls and boys involving cacao. The ritual was conducted by gathering the children within a cord held by four men representing the elements of *Chac* (the rain god), each standing in a corner of the room. Then the high priest took a bone and wet it in a vessel filled with water made of "certain flowers and of cacao pounded and dissolved in virgin water…". With this liquid he anointed the children on their foreheads, faces, and in the spaces between the fingers and toes, in complete silence.

Another ritual was practiced in the Yucatan region. The sinkhole (*cenote*) gardens of the Yucatan peninsula were of little economic significance, however local Yucatan cacao commanded enough respect to have its own special ritual as described by the archeologist Landa: "In the month of *Muan*, those who owned cacao plantations celebrated a festival to the gods *Ek Chuah*, *Chac* and *Hobnil*, who were their mediators. To solemnize it they went to some plantation belonging to one of their number, where they sacrificed a dog, spotted with the colour of cacao, and they burned their incense to their idols and offered them iguanas of a blue colour, and certain feathers of a bird, and other kinds of game, and they gave to each of the officials a spike of the fruit of the cacao (presumably a cacao pod)."

The Mayans were the first major civilisation to use cacao as currency. The Mayans even had cacao god(s). Some of the Mayan deity names associated with cacao include:

- *Chac* (the rain god, associated with cacao)
- *Hobnil*
- *Ek Chuah* (also considered the God of Merchants who had with him a cacao tree and protected cacao growers and traders)

The Aztecs, who rose after the collapse of the Mayan civilisation, adapted cacao into their civilisation. They associated cacao with the Aztec Lord of the Flowers, *Xochipilli*, god of song, poetry, and springtime and his counterpart *Xochiquetzal*, the goddess of flowers. In the Aztec sacred cosmological map of the cosmos, the cacao tree occupies the space of one the great world trees.

To the Aztecs the consumption of cacao became ritualistic. Cacao was often

Xochipilli on a Mexican 100 peso note

associated with wealth, prestige and nobility. Marriages among the Aztecs involved an exchange of bride to groom and groom to bride of five cacao beans.

Near the Aztec capital of Tenochtitlan, at the ancient pyramids of Teotihuacan, we find a mural depicting a cacao tree in Tlalocan, the paradise of the rain gods. The murals discovered at the Mexican pyramid in Cholula also depict cacao.

A famous historical European encounter with cacao took place when Columbus came across a large Aztec-controlled Yucatan trading canoe with cacao beans amongst its cargo. Columbus and his crew noted that when one of the natives dropped a cacao bean, they frantically scrambled to pick it up. Columbus thought this was strange as he assumed cacao beans were almonds; he was unaware that cacao beans were money to these people as they had been to the Maya before them.

The future of cacao shifted dramatically when conquistador Hernan Cortes landed his fleet in what is now Veracruz, Mexico on Good Friday, April 22, 1519. Cortes was sailing, against orders, from Cuba. The ruling Aztecs and many of the other tribes believed Cortes was the god *Quetzalcoatl* returning

Hernan Cortes

from over the seas. Through what has to be one of the most intriguing stories in history, Cortes, with the help of native peoples (who resented Aztec rule) and Malinche (a young native Mesoamerican female interpreter), eventually captured the extraordinary Aztec capital city of Tenochtitlan (now Mexico City) and took the Aztec Emperor Montezuma hostage on August 13th, 1521. With Montezuma deposed, Cortes suddenly was the ruler of a large portion of what is politically, today, central Mexico. This area stretched from the Caribbean to the Pacific Ocean.

The deposed Aztec Emperor Montezuma was a confirmed chocoholic (chocolate lover/addict). Bernal Diaz del Castillo, a soldier in Cortes' army who recorded, in his famous memoirs, an account of one of Montezuma's great feasts: "From time to time, they brought him, in cup-shaped vessels of pure gold, a certain drink made from cacao, and the women served this drink to him with great reverence." Montezuma, according to Bernal Diaz del Castillo, would serve at the feasts "...over two thousand jugs of cacao all frothed up..." Rumor had it that Montezuma would consume 50 cups of the cacao drink before visiting his harem.

When political turmoil caused Cortes to return to Spain in 1528, he brought with him precious minerals, agricultural goods and, most likely, cacao beans with their attendant praises. Cortes was probably the first to bring chocolate to Europe and the world would never be the same.

About the cacao drink, Cortes wrote: "The divine drink which builds up resistance and fights fatigue. A cup of this precious drink permits a man to walk for a whole day without food."

Chocolate Today

It was the Europeans who eventually combined cacao with refined sugar; the native Americans always preferred bitter chocolate. We now know that refined sugar draws minerals out of the body, causes blood sugar disorders, dehydration, and is highly addictive. Sugar with all its attendant dangers lowered the medicinal value of the chocolate sold in Europe and altered the spirit of cacao's original intent of being a healing food.

In 1828, a Dutch chemist named Coenraad Johannes Van Houten received a patent on a process for the manufacture of a new kind of low-fat powdered chocolate. As early as 1815, in his own Amsterdam factory, he had been looking for a better method than boiling and skimming to remove most of the cacao butter from chocolate. He eventually developed a very efficient hydraulic press that squeezed the oil out of the cacao. Cacao typically contains around 50 percent cacao oil/butter, but when the cacao was processed through Van Houten's machine the cacao

prenez du Cacao
Van Houten

was reduced to around 27 percent oil/butter leaving a "cake" that could be pulverised into a fine powder. Van Houten created what would eventually be termed "cocoa or cocoa powder." To cause his cocoa powder to mix well with water, Van Houten treated it with alkaline salts (potassium or sodium carbonates). While this "Dutching," as it came to be known, improved the powder's miscibility (not its solubility) in warm water, it also made the chocolate darker in colour and milder in flavour.

Van Houten's invention of the defatting and alkalising processes made it possible to develop large-scale manufacturing and distribution of cheap chocolate for millions of people in powdered and solid forms.

The invention of notoriously-problematic milk chocolate was due to the collective effort of two men: the Swiss chemist Henri Nestlé (1814-1890) and Swiss chocolate manufacturer Daniel Peter (1836-1919). In 1867, Nestlé discovered a process to powder milk by evaporation. This discovery eventually made Nestlé's business enterprise the largest food corporation in the world. It was Daniel Peter who came up with the idea of using Nestlé's milk powder in a new kind of chocolate. In 1879, the first milk chocolate bar was produced.

Although considered a monumental moment in food history, it was the addition of powdered milk that blocked the healing antioxidant properties of cacao from being effective as we shall explore in our discussion of cacao's antioxidants.

Money Does Grow On Trees

"Oompa-Loompas!" everyone said at once. "Oompa-Loompas!"

"Imported direct from Loompaland," said Mr Wonka proudly.

"There's no such place," said Mrs Salt.

"Excuse me, dear lady, but ..."

"Mr Wonka," cried Mrs Salt. "I am a teacher of geography ..."

"Then you'll know all about it," said Mr Wonka. "And oh, what a terrible country it is! Nothing but thick jungles infested by the most dangerous beasts in the entire world — hornswogglers and snozzwangers and those terrible wicked whangdoodles. A whangdoodle would eat ten Oompa-Loompas for breakfast and come galloping back for a second helping. When I went out there, I found the little Oompa-Loompas living in tree-houses. They had to live in tree-houses to escape from the whangdoodles and the hornswogglers and the snozzwangers. And they were practically starving to death. They were living on green caterpillars, and the caterpillars tasted revolting, and the Oompa-Loompas spent every moment of their days climbing through the treetops looking for other things to mash up with the caterpillars to make them taste better — red beetles, for instance, and eucalyptus leaves, and the bark of the bong-bong tree, all of them beastly, but not quite so beastly as the caterpillars. Poor little Oompa-Loompas! The one food that they longed for more than any other was the cacao bean. But they couldn't get it. An Oompa-Loompa was lucky if he found three or four cacao beans a year. But oh, how they craved them. They used to dream about cacao beans all night and talk about them all day. You had only to mention the word 'cacao' to an Oompa-Loompa and he would start dribbling at the mouth. The cacao bean," Mr Wonka continued, "which grows on the cacao tree, happens to be the thing from which all chocolate is made. You cannot make chocolate without the cacao bean. The cacao bean is chocolate. I myself use billions of cacao beans every week in this factory. And so, my dear children, as soon as I discovered that the Oompa-Loompas were crazy for this particular food, I climbed up to their tree-house village and poked my head in through the door of the tree house belonging to the leader of the tribe. The poor little fellow, looking thin and starved, was sitting there trying to eat a bowl full of mashed-up green caterpillars without being sick. "Look here," I said (speaking not in English, of course, but in Oompa-Loompish), "look here, if you and all your people will come back to my country and live in my factory, you can have all the cacao beans you want! I've got mountains of them in my storehouses! You can have cacao beans for every meal! You can gorge yourselves silly on them! I'll even pay your wages in cacao beans if you wish!" — **Charlie and the Chocolate Factory** by Roald Dahl, Chapter 16: *Oompa-Loompas.*

We are always amazed at how many people know about the Oompa-Loompas. Having been made famous through the magnficent songs of the film: *Willie Wonka and the Chocolate Factory* (1971), the Oompa-Loompas have been a mainstay of American culture ever since. However, nobody seems to know what the Oompa-Loompas eat (cacao beans!) or why they came to Willy Wonka's factory (cacao beans!). Everyone should read Roald Dahl's classic book!

Cacao beans are simply the seed of the cacao fruit. They may be referred to as cacao beans, cacao seeds, cacao nuts, chocolate seeds, chocolate beans or cacao nibs — all mean the same thing. For simplicity, we usually use the term "cacao beans."

Edible Money

"But it is very needfull to heare what happie money they use, for they have money, which I call happy, because for the greedie desire and gaping to attaine the same, the bowelles of the earth are not rent a sunder, nor through the ravening greediness of covetous men, nor terrour of warres assayling, it returneth to the dennes and caves of the mother earth, as golden, or silver money doth. For this groweth upon trees." — Peter Martyr (Pietro Martire D'Anghiera, Milanese chronicler who coined the phrase "The New World") from **De Orbe Novo** (1530)

In ancient Central American cultures, raw cacao beans were actually used as money. Imagine an edible money! As fantastic as the Valley of Mexico appeared to Hernan Cortes and his men, as incredible as the civilization before them appeared, nothing was so strange as the coin of the realm — not gold or silver — but cacao beans...by the millions. When the Spanish came to understand the value of cacao beans, they called them black gold (*oro negro*) or seeds of gold (*pepe de oro*).

Montezuma (*Motecuhzoma Xocoyotzin*), the emperor of the great city of Tenochtitlan (now Mexico city) and of the Aztec empire, had his treasure vaults filled with cacao beans, not gold! The chronicler Francisco Cervantes de Salazar mentions that the Emperor's cacao warehouse held more than 40,000 loads, which would mean 960,000,000 beans!

Montezuma paid his military, workers, civil servants, etc. in cacao. One of Cortes' soldiers, Bernal Diaz del Castillo, recorded that more than 2,000 containers of chocolate drink were daily destined for the soldiers of Montezuma's palace guard!

The normal load of cacao in the backpack of a trader or porter was three *xiquipillis*, or 24,000 beans, called a *carga* by the Spanish. Each *xiquipil*, of course, contained 8,000 beans. Each *carga* was carried to the Aztec capital Tenochtitlan from cacao farms located hundreds of kilometres from the capital city. These cacao farms were in Aztec controlled lands and paid the Aztecs in tribute as much as 40% of the cacao beans they produced. Thus a farm producing 50 *xiquipillis* could pay as much as 20 *xiquipillis* in tribute and be left to use the remaining cacao to pay for labour, to trade and to eat.

In the city of Texcoco, near Tenochtitlan, the poet-king Nezahualcoyotl paid out as much as 32,000 cacao beans a day as the city budget demanded. At that rate, Nezahualcoyotl would have spent 11,680,000 beans annually, or just over 486 loads.

Since the emperor and his staff controlled the importation and distribution of cacao beans into the realm, and because there was no banking (charging interest on money), inflation and erratic money dynamics were unknown.

Nezahualcoyotl, the poet-king on the Mexican 100 peso note

The chronicler Motolinia tells us that in his day (shortly after Cortes' conquest of Tenochtitlan), the daily wage of a porter in central Mexico was 100 beans, which puts into perspective the following partial list of commodity prices in Tlaxcala, from a Nahuatl document circa 1545:

- One good turkey hen is worth 100 full cacao beans, or 120 shrunken beans.
- A turkey cock is worth 200 cacao beans.
- A hare [jackrabbit] or forest rabbit is worth 100 cacao beans each.
- A small rabbit is worth 30 cacao beans.
- One turkey egg is worth 3 cacao beans.
- An avocado newly picked is worth 3 cacao beans; when an avocado is fully ripe it is equivalent to one cacao bean.
- One large tomato is equivalent to a cacao bean.
- Five green chilies is equivalent to a cacao bean.
- A large sapote fruit, or two small ones, is equivalent to a cacao bean.
- A large axolotl [larval salamander, an Aztec delicacy] is worth 4 cacao beans, a small one is worth 2 or 3 cacao beans.
- A tamale is exchanged for a cacao bean.
- Fish wrapped in maize husks is worth 3 cacao beans.

On market day, between 65 and 300 beans bought you a hand-made cotton cloak. With 100 beans, one could purchase a dugout canoe or even a slave.

23

As with any currency system, counterfeiting of cacao was common. Phony cacao beans could be made of amaranth dough, beeswax and pieces of avocado seeds. Even though counterfeiting was punishable by death, the cacao bean was so valuable that it was worth the risk!

Cacao beans continued to be used as standard currency in Mexico until 1887.

Under the most favourable conditions cacao beans cannot be preserved for more than three years. This makes for an ideal money as, by its nature, it must be used and put into the flow of commerce. Cacao literally carries the energy of prosperity without hoarding. Peter Martyr D'Angheira in his revered text **De Orbo Novo** (1530) wrote: "O blessed money, which not only gives to the human race a useful and delightful drink, but also prevents its possessors from yielding to internal avarice, for it cannot be piled up, or hoarded for a long time."

Cacao is wealth. Cacao embodies the energy of abundance and opportunity. Built into the cacao bean is the possibility to go from longshot to legend, from depression to profound optimism, the possibility of being the lottery winner, the possibility of going from rags to riches. This is the special, unique energy that makes cacao the most powerful food on Earth.

Preparing Edible Money

Typical preparation of cacao beans involves the removal of the fruit pulp with seeds from the fruit husks (outer rind) onto large leaves *in situ*, then natural sprouting with attendant fermentation of the fruit pulp along with the seeds would occur; this is followed by collecting and drying the seeds. The ancient technique was to lay out large leaves on the floor of the jungle, then pour all the pulp with seeds onto the leaves; after 3 to 5 days, the pulp would heat up and the seed would momentarily sprout as the pulp fermented. The cacao seeds were then ready for sun drying, which could take a couple of weeks. With more efficient processing techniques today, high-quality cacao beans can be removed from the fruit shells and then dried in one day with as low as a 15% fruit fermentation rate which makes for a better tasting raw bean.

During the fermentation process, the fruit pulp surrounding the seeds liquifies into a vinegar, alcohol-like solution and drains away over the seeds. As this occurs the temperature of the fermenting beans steadily increases. The seeds briefly germinate releasing amino acids, creating a stronger chocolate flavour. However, the seeds do not make it far as they are soon overwhelmed by the increased acidity of the fermenting vinegar. For several days, this

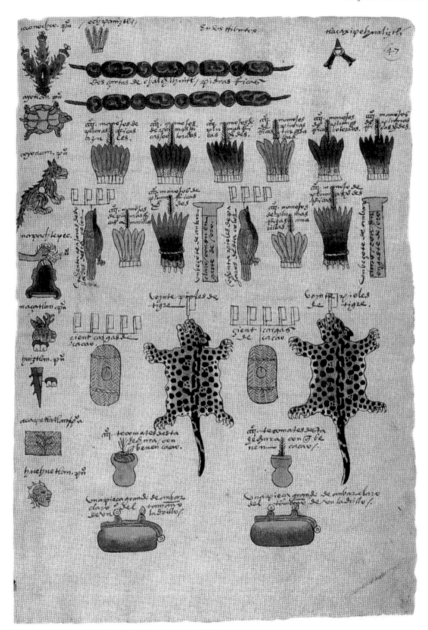

This folio from the sixteenth-century Códice Mendoza records the tributes paid to the Aztec rulers twice a year by the subject cacao-growing region of Xoconochco (Shoconoshco). Besides jaguar skins, cotinga feathers and the prized green stone *chalchihuitl*. Xoconochco provided Tenochtitlán with 200 loads of freshly harvested cacao and 800 gourds to drink chocolate. According to the sixteenth-century Spanish chronicler Fray Toribio de Benavente (Motolinia), a load of cacao was equivalent to 24,000 beans. — **The New Taste Of Chocolate**

process continues as the beans are turned over a few times throughout each day in an effort to keep the fermenting beans at a temperature between 45 degrees C (113°F) and 50 degrees C (122°F) so as to keep enzymes active and draw out the perfect flavour.

During fermentation of the beans, enzymes "chew" on the proteins, freeing the amino acids. The amino acids are the "flavour precursors," meaning they give rise to flavour compounds characteristic of the chocolate we know and love.

If cacao is roasted this can also affect flavour. With heating, the freed amino acids combine with sugars and other elements to create compounds that create different taste sensations. For instance, the sulphur-containing amino acid methionine undergoes a reaction to produce 3-methiopro-panal, which has a sulphurous character. The amino acid leucine produces isovaleraldehyde, which has a fruity character.

After fermentation, the beans are spread onto mats to dry in the sun. Drying may take several weeks.

The processing of cacao beans is similar to the process of water-soaking, then dehydrating nuts and seeds (common in raw-food or living-food cuisine) so as to increase availability of proteins in the form of freed amino acids and to lower enzyme inhibitors.

When processed and dried, cacao is tremendously hardy in all different kinds of environments and climates. It is resistant to mold. The hardy, anti-fungal cacao skin protects the treat inside.

The processing and drying process allowed cacao to travel far, last long and work wonderfully as currency. Imagine a cacao bean passing through many hands, and then, when the time was ripe, one could peel off the dirty exterior and enjoy the treat inside!

For food purposes, cacao beans do not have to be processed, they can be eaten straight out of the fruit or quickly dried with fruit pulp on them (making a tasty treat). When untreated in this way, they have less chocolaty flavour, yet seemingly stronger psychoactive properties (higher levels of neurotransmitter enhancing activity). Additionally, the purple antioxidant colour is more pronounced in these unsprouted, unfermented beans.

Ideas and mythology relating to cacao beans having to be fermented and/or cooked to be edible are completely absurd. However, these rumours still abound and indicate how much mystery surrounds this incredible tree, its fruit and seed. It seems clear, based on the insights of raw-food nutrition, that cacao was discovered by ancient humans in the South and/or Central American jungles. They ate it raw initially for its fruit pulp, and then later found that even a small quantity of fresh raw seeds (five or six) imparted energising, magical qualities upon the consumer. In a situation where it is difficult to procure food and where one cacao fruit, with its fruits and seeds, can feed a group, it is no wonder that cacao came into general cultivation and subsequent alchemical experimentation.

In unfermented cacao beans, pigment cells make up about 11-13% of the tissue. The pigment cells contain approximately 65-70% antioxidant polyphenols which is about 6% to 8% by weight of the dried bean (polyphenols include catechins, the same antioxidant found in green tea) and 3% antioxidant anthocyanins by weight. During fermentation the polyphenols undergo a variety of reactions, including self-condensation and reaction with proteins and peptides. Approximately 20% of the polyphenols by weight remain at the end of the fermentation process. The level of polyphenols will vary with the variety of cacao bean and with the degree of fermentation.

The catechins are colourless. The anthocyanins are of a purple colour and are strongly present in the unfermented beans. During fermentation and drying the purple anthocyanins are converted to quinonic compounds to give the bean its characteristic brown colour.

Selecting Quality Money

The best cacao beans are large (bigger than large almonds and almost as big as a Brazil nut), rotund, heavy and smooth with a papery, easy to peel skin.

The sixteenth-century Códice Azoyu is a pictoral chronicle of the political history and chronology of the small kingdom of Tlachinollan, in today's Guerrero state in Mexico. — **The New Taste Of Chocolate**

Montezuma

Colour

Chocolate beans vary in colour from rich whites, purples, reds, coppers, metallic grays, as well as the more common shades of browns fading into dark black. We have had tasty cacaos with no colour. Colour is not necessarily a sign of quality. Darker chocolate is not necessarily better as common assumptions indicate.

Taste

With a clean palette put a peeled cacao bean in your mouth and let it linger on your tongue for a short while and slowly move it around hinting at all the flavours. As you crunch into the bean, the main point to look for is solid crunch. If the first bean is dull and soft, then the bean has been sitting somewhere for a while — the bean is stale. The second main point is to look for transformations of flavour over the first twenty bites. Generally, premium quality beans will show three to five elements of flavour. Lesser quality beans show one to two elements of flavour.

The overall taste should be cooling, subtly dry, fatty with natural sweetness, slightly bitter with low astringency, low vinegar sensations with a very slight, distant, waxy texture.

Avoid eating too many beans that show shifting tastes of acidity leading to mouth sores (caused by an excess of the amino acid arginine).

Texture

Generally speaking, a shiny smooth bean texture with an absence of any mold is the mark of a good cacao. As you peel the cacao bean, it may crumble into nibs, this is no cause for alarm, the bean is still of high quality.

Once the cacao bean is peeled watch for signs of white or green mold. Contamination is usually obvious.

When the inner kernels are separated from the shells (skins), they should be shiny while displaying various colours.

White Chocolate

Today white chocolate is made out of cacao butter only (the fat of cacao seeds) and it contains no cacao seed solids. Originally, however, white chocolate was made with white cacao beans. These are cacao beans with low antioxidant content and little colour. They resemble to some degree the inner colour of an almond. These white cacaos are genetic mutants and are not bred today.

Cacao Shells/Skins

The cacao shell/skin is the outer paper-like covering around the seed. They are a common article of commerce, being used as garden fertiliser due to their 10% nitrogen content and in preparing a tea resembling chocolate or cacao in taste, but being naturally weaker than these.

Traditional methods of drying, handling, and distributing cacao usually meant that the skins were contaminated by bacteria. Therefore, peeling the skin before eating has been the common practice. One of the primary reasons cacao was cooked was to make it easy to remove the skin. Now with technology, well-prepared organic cacao beans are available with low bacteria counts on the skin. Beware however, not all organic cacao beans have clean skins. If unsure, peel your cacao beans or purchase raw cacao nibs.

Chocolate Toothpaste

There has long been an association with chocolate and the health of the teeth. We find, for example, that Charlie Bucket's father in the book **Charlie and The Chocolate Factory** works in a toothpaste factory! We have insight as to why this is because once one starts eating cacao beans, one may be attracted to using sweeteners such as honey or agave cactus syrup to draw out the extraordinary taste. Yet, one has to be careful, because too much sweetener is not good for the teeth.

Aztec ruler giving chocolate to Neptune

Interestingly, cacao itself is actually good for the teeth. The consumption of cacao with the skins seems to decrease cavities. Research has shown that the tannins in the cacao and its skin prevent tooth decay. The following experiments are conclusive in this regard:

"Cariostatic Activity of Cacao Mass Extract" by Ooshima T, Osaka Y, Sasaki H, Osawa K, Yasuda H, Matsumoto M, Departments of Pedodontics, Osaka University Faculty of Dentistry, 1-8 Yamadaoka, Suita, 565-0871, Osaka, Japan. **Arch Oral Biol** 2000 Sep; 45(9):805-8

Abstract

Chocolate is suspected to contain some caries-inhibitory substances. The cariostatic activity of cacao mass extract (CM), the main component of chocolate, was examined in vitro and in experimental animals. CM showed no detectable effects on the cellular growth and acid production of *mutans streptococci*. On the other hand, the cell-surface hydrophobicity of *mutans streptococci* was significantly reduced by the presence of CM. Furthermore, insoluble glucan synthesis by the glucosyltransferases from either *Streptococcus mutans MT8148R* or *Strep. sobrinus 6715* was inhibited by CM, but not significantly. Hence, the sucrose-dependent cell adherence of *mutans streptococci* was also depressed by CM. Finally, CM in both a 40% sucrose diet and drinking water resulted in reductions of caries development and plaque accumulation in rats infected with *Strep. sobrinus 6715*, but not significantly. These results indicate that cacao mass extract possesses some anticariogenic potential, but its anticaries activity is not strong enough to suppress significantly the cariogenic activity of sucrose.

"Identification of Cariostatic Substances in the Cacao Bean Husk: Their Anti-Glucosyltransferase and Antibacterial Activities" by Osawa K, Miyazaki K, Shimura S, Okuda J, Matsumoto M, Ooshima T. Central Laboratory, Lotte Co. Ltd., Saitama, Saitama, Japan. **J Dent Res**. 2001 Nov;80(11):2000-4.

Abstract

The cacao bean husk has been shown to possess two types of cariostatic substances, one showing anti-glucosyltransferase (GTF) activity and the other antibacterial activity, and to inhibit experimental dental caries in rats infected with *Streptococci mutans*.

In the present study, chromatographic purification revealed high-molecular-weight polyphenolic compounds and unsaturated fatty acids as active components. The former, which showed strong anti-GTF activity, were polymeric epicatechins with C-4beta and C-8 intermolecular bonds estimated to be 4636 in molecular weight in an acetylated form. The latter, which showed bactericidal activity against *Streptococcus mutans*, were determined to be oleic and linoleic acids, and demonstrated a high level of activity at a concentration of 30 microgram/mL. The cariostatic activity of the cacao bean husk is likely caused by these biologically active constituents.

According to research cited by Jonathan Ott in his book, **The Cacahuatl Eater: Ruminations Of An Unabashed Chocolate Addict**, the results of the Vipeholm Dental Caries Study indicate that chocolate consumption is not associated with tooth decay. In this study, 436 adult inmates of a Swedish mental institution were divided into several groups receiving different, yet controlled diets over a five-year period, during which the incidence of tooth decay was monitored. There was a "chocolate group" whose members each received 65 grams of milk chocolate daily between meals, with no significant rise in dental decay. Additionally, 77 employees of the mental institution were given 54 grams of milk chocolate daily between meals, again with no observed increase in tooth decay.

Also, according to Ott, experiments conducted by Stralfors showed that theobromine (which we will see in Part II is a major active principle in cacao), at a level of 0.2% in the diet of hamsters, inhibited the incidence of cavities by 37% compared to controls fed the same diet without theo-bromine.

The Old World meets The New World and the gift of cacao beans are exchanged.

Part II: Scientific Properties of Chocolate

"It's not that chocolates are a substitute for love. Love is a substitute for chocolate. Chocolate is, let's face it, far more reliable than a man..."
— Miranda Ingram

Chemical Composition of Cacao

Substances in chocolate that have been discussed in the scientific literature as pharmacologically significant, include: anandamide, arginine, epicatechins, histamine, magnesium, phenylethylamine (PEA), polyphenols, salsolinol, serotonin, theobromine, tryptophan, tyramine and vitamin C. Of course some of these exist in higher concentrations in other foods, but other foods have much less appeal than chocolate!

The Cacao Bean's Natural Chemical Constituents and Their Concentrations (when available):

3-ALPHA-L-ARABINOSIDYL-CYANIDIN

3-BETA-D-GALACTOSIDYL-CYANIDIN

4-HYDROXY-3-METHOXY-BENZOIC-ACID

3-METHYLOXYTYRAMINE

ACETIC-ACID 1,520 - 7,100 ppm

ALANINE 10,400 ppm

ALKALOIDS 33,900 ppm

ALPHA-THEOSTEROL

AMYL-ACETATE

AMYL-ALCOHOL

AMYL-BUTYRATE

AMYLASE

ANANDAMIDE

ARABINOSE

ARGININE 800+ ppm

ASCORBIC-ACID 31 ppm

ASCORBIC-ACID-OXIDASE

ASPARIGINASE

BETA-THEOSTEROL

CAFFEIC-ACID

CAFFEINE Petiole 51 - 525 ppm or 500 - 12,900 ppm , Skin 130 - 723 ppm

CALCIUM 800 - 1,100 ppm

CAMPOSTEROL

CARBOHYDRATES 347,000 - 445,000 ppm

CATALASE

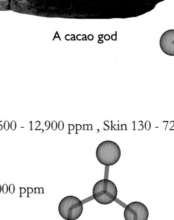

A cacao god

CATECHINS 30,000 - 35,000 ppm

CHLORIDE 120 ppm

CHROMIUM (10 times more than whole wheat, highest of any major food)

CITRIC-ACID 4,500 - 7,500 ppm

COPPER 24 ppm

COUMARIN

CYANIDIN-3-BETA-L-ARABINOSIDE

CYANIDIN-3-GALACTOSIDE

CYANIDIN-GLYCOSIDE 4,000 - 5,000 ppm

DOPAMINE

EPIGALLOCATECHIN

ERGOSTEROL

ESCULETIN

FAT 371,000 - 582,300 ppm

FERULIC-ACID

FIBER 59,000 - 89,000 ppm

FORMIC-ACID

FURFUROL

GLUCOSE 3,000 ppm

GLUTAMIC-ACID 10,200 ppm

GLYCINE 900 ppm

HISTAMINE

HISTIDINE 800 ppm

INVERTASE

IRON 36 - 37 ppm

IRON-OXIDE 40 ppm

ISOBUTYL-ACETATE

ISOLEUCINE 5,600 ppm

L-EPICATECHIN 27,000 ppm

LACTIC-ACID

LEUCINE

LEUCOCYANIDINS 14,000 - 35,000 ppm

LINALOL 5 ppm

LINOLEIC-ACID

LINOLENIC-ACID

A cacao god

35

LIPASE

LYSINE 800 ppm

LYSOPHOSPHATIDYLCHOLINE

MAGNESIUM

MANNAN

MANNINOTRIOSE

MANNOSE

MELIBIOSE

MESO-INOSITOL

METHYLTETRAHYDROISOQUINOLINE

METHYL-HEPTENONE

N-BUTYLACETATE

N-LINOLEOYLETHANOLAMINE — Anandamide reuptake inhibitor

N-NONACOSANE

N-OLEOLETHANOLAMINE — Anandamide reuptake inhibitor

NIACIN 17 - 18 ppm

NICOTINAMIDE 21 ppm

NITROGEN 22,800 ppm

NONANOIC-ACID

O-HYDROXYPHENYLACETIC-ACID

OCTOIC-ACID

OLEIC-ACID 190,000 - 217,000 ppm

OLEO-DIPALMATIN 76,500 - 92,800 ppm

OLEOPALMITOSTEARIN

OXALIC-ACID 1,520 - 5,000 ppm

P-ANISIC-ACID

P-COUMARIC-ACID

P-HYDROXY-BENZOIC-ACID

P-HYDROXYPHENYLACETIC-ACID

P-TYRAMINE

PALMITIC-ACID

PALMITODIOLEN

PANTOTHENIC-ACID (Vitamin B5) 13 ppm

PECTIN

PENTOSE

PEROXIDASE

A cacao god

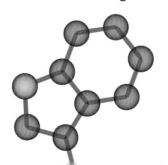

PHENYLACETIC-ACID

PHENYLALANINE 5,600 ppm

PHENYLETHYLAMINE

PHOSPHATIDYL-CHOLINE 92 - 1,328 ppm

PHOSPHOLIPIDS

PHOSPHORUS 3,600 - 5,571 ppm

POLYPHENOLS 78,000 - 100,000 ppm

PROLINE 7,200 ppm

PROPIONIC-ACID

PROTEIN 120,000 - 180,000 ppm

PROTEINASE

PROTOCATECHUIC-ACID

PURINE 30,000 - 40,000 ppm

PYRIDOXINE (Vitamin B6) 1 ppm

RIBOFLAVIN (Vitamin B2) 1 - 4 ppm

SALSOLINOL

SERINE 8,800 ppm

SEROTONIN

SITOSTEROL

SPERMIDINE

SPERMINE

STACHYOSE

STARCH 60,000 ppm

STEARIC-ACID

STEARODIOLEIN

STIGMASTEROL

SYRINGIC-ACID

TANNINS 75,400 ppm

TARTARIC-ACID

TELEMETHYLHISTAMINE

THEOBROMINE 10,000 - 33,500 ppm

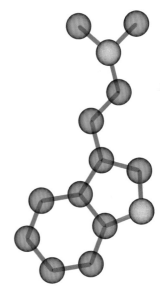

THEOPHYLLINE 3,254 - 4,739 ppm — Theophylline is a methyl-xanthine with diuretic and bronchial smooth muscle relaxant properties.

THIAMINE (vitamin B1) 1 - 3 ppm

THREONINE 1,400 ppm

TOCOPHEROL (BETA, GAMMA) (vitamin E forms)

TRIGONELLINE

TRYPTOPHAN

TYRAMINE

TYROSINE 5,700 ppm

VALERIANIC-ACID

VALERIC-ACID

VALINE 5,700 ppm

VANILLIC-ACID

VERBASCOSE

VERBASCOTETROSE

WATER 36,000 ppm

XYLOSE

NOTE: The ppm (parts per million) values listed above will not add up to 1,000,000 as some constituents contain the other (e.g,. protein contains glycine), the information is derived from many different studies, and the natural variation of nutrients.

Average Cacao Bean Chemistry (per 100 grams)

456 calories

3.6 g H_2O

12.0 g protein

46.3 g fat (typically 40 to 50 grams, but sometimes as low as 12 grams)

34.7 g total carbohydrate (starch ranges from 1.3 to 7.5 grams according to Ridenour, **Amer. Jour. Pharm.**, 1895, p. 209)

8.6 g fiber (albuminous matter ranges from 6 to 18 grams)

3.4 g ash

106 mg calcium

537 mg phosphorus

3.6 mg Fe (iron)

0.17-0.24 mg thiamine

0.14-0.41 mg riboflavin

1.7 mg niacin

2.1 mg nicotinamide

1.35 mg pantothenic acid

0.09 mg pyridoxine

3.0 mg ascorbic acid

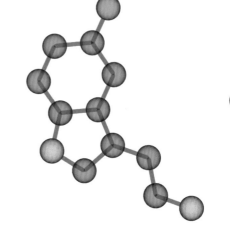

Unfermented Versus Fermented Cacao Beans

The Individual Amino Acids In The Water-Soluble Fractions of Unfermented and Fermented Beans are (in grams per 100 grams):

Compound	Unfermented	Fermented
lysine	0.08	0.56
histidine	0.08	0.04
arginine	0.08	0.03
threonine	0.14	0.84
serine	0.88	1.99
glutamic acid	1.02	1.77
proline	0.72	1.97
glycine	0.09	0.35
alanine	1.04	3.61
valine	0.57	2.60
isoleucine	0.56	1.68
leucine	0.45	4.75
tyrosine	0.57	1.27
phenylalanine	0.56	3.36

Unfermented and Fermented Beans Contain

p-hydroxybenzoic acid

vanillic acid

p-coumaric acid

ferulic acid

syringic acid

The Fermented Beans Also Contain

protocatechuic

phenylacetic

phloretic acid

esculetin (a lactone)

o- and p-hydroxyphenyl acids

The Unfermented Beans Also Contain

Caffeic acid

Fruit Pulp

According to the Wealth of India, the Edible Pulp of the Fruit Contains

79.7 to 88.5% water

0.5 to 0.7% albuminoids, astringents, etc.

8.3 to 13.1% glucose

0.4 to 0.9% sucrose

A trace of starch

0.2 to 0.4% non-volatile acids (as tartaric)

0.03% Fe_2O_3

0.4% mineral salts (K, Na, Ca, Mg)

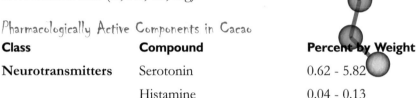

Pharmacologically Active Components in Cacao

Class	Compound	Percent by Weight
Neurotransmitters	Serotonin	0.62 - 5.82
	Histamine	0.04 - 0.13
Methylxanthines	Theobromine	< 1.3
	Caffeine	not detected
Tetrahydroisoquinolines	Salsolinol	High
	Methyltetrahydroisoquinoline	< 0.01
Amines	Phenylethylamine	0.02 - 2.20
	Tele-methylhistamine	0.01 - 1.54
	Spermidine	0.05 - 1.15
	p-tyramine	0.02 - 0.35
	3-methyloxytyramine	0.02 - 0.33
	Tryptamine	0.03 - 0.18
	Spermine	0.00 - 0.13

Source: **Biochemist**, Apr/May 1993, p 15.

The Fatty Acid Components of Cocoa Butter Include

20-30% palmitic and lower acids (16:0)

30-35% stearic and higher acids (18:0)

30-35% oleic acid (18:1)

2-4% linoleic (18:2) (omega 6 fatty acid)

0-0.3% linolenic (18:3) (omega 3 fatty acid)

Unique Lipids In Cacao Beans

Cocoa butter contains mainly beta- and gamma-tocopherols (vitamin E forms) in the range of 150-250 mg/gram.

Polar lipids make up 1-2% of the cacao bean. Of these polar lipids two-thirds are glycolipids and one-third are phospholipids and phytosterols. Phytosterols are found in concentrations of 1.8 to 2 mg/gram and are composed of sitosterol (50-70%), stigmasterol (20-30%) and camposterol (5-9%).

For more information on understanding fats and oils in food, please reference Udo Erasmus' book **Fats That Heal, Fats That Kill**.

Cocoa Powder

Cocoa Powder Contains Over 300 Volatile Compounds, Including

Esters

Hydrocarbons

Lactones

Monocarbonyls

Pyrazines

Pyrroles

The Important Flavour Components Include

Aliphatic esters
Polyphenols (antioxidants)
Unsaturated aromatic carbonyls
Pyrazines
Diketopiperazines
Theobromine

Cocoa Powder Also Contains

18% Proteins (8% digestible)
Fats (cocoa butter)

Amines and Alkaloids, including:

Theobromine (0.5 to 2.7%)
Caffeine (0.25% in cocoa; 0.7 to 1.70 in fat-free beans, with *forasteros* containing less than 0.1% and *criollos* containing 1.43 to 1.70%)
Tyramine
Dopamine
Salsolinol
Trigonelline

Nicotinic acid

Free amino acids

Tannins

Phospholipids

According to Jonathan Ott in his book **The Cacahuatl Eater: Ruminations Of An Unabashed Chocolate Addict**, 100 grams of Cocoa Contains:

550 mg magnesium

3.6 mg copper

7.6 mg zinc

3.8 mg manganese

0.17 mg pyridoxine

0.33 mg pantothenic acid

0.2 mg vitamin E

Cacao Shells/Skins

The Average Cacao Shell Contains

11.0% moisture

3.0% fat

13.5% protein

16.5% crude fiber

9.0% tannins

6.0% pentosans

6.5% ash

0.75% theobromine

The remaining percentages were unspecified in this report.

Cacao Shells/Skins Were Found by T. S. Clarkson To Contain

0.9% alkaloids (theobromine, caffeine)

10.9% nitrogenous matter

5.32% fat

5.6% mucilage

9.07% ash containing aluminum

A resin soluble in ether and alcohol, and having the odour of cacao.

In addition to alkaloids (mainly theobromine), tannins and other constituents, cocoa shells/skins contain a pigment that is a polyflavone glucoside with a molecular weight of over 1500; this pigment is claimed to be heat and light resistant, highly stable at pH 3 to 11, and useful as a food colourant; it was isolated at a 7.9% yield (Leung, 1980).

Magnesium

As students of nutrition, we are convinced that the primary components of foods that influence feelings of health, well-being, nourishment and satisfaction are minerals. We believe that any conversation about nutrition can first begin with a study of minerals because the primary mineral or minerals contained in a food reveal much about its magic.

Magnesium is the most deficient major mineral in the diet of civilisation and yet is one of the most important of all minerals. Over 80% of the United States' population is deficient in magnesium.

An ancient pyramid at Teotihuacan, Mexico

Sources of Magnesium

In nature, the primary source of magnesium is cacao (raw chocolate beans)! Other sources of magnesium include seaweeds such as kelp and dulse, unprocessed wheat seeds, sunflower seeds, almonds, cashews, chlorophyll-rich green vegetables, micro-algae (chlorella, spirulina, AFA blue-green algae, marine phytoplankton), cleansing fruits such as cassia (senna), and/or sea salts. Notably, magnesium is found at the centre of the chlorophyll molecule.

Due to its unusually high content of alkaline magnesium, cacao is the most alkaline of all nuts. Cacao contains more magnesium than almonds do calcium.

Magnesium supports the heart, increases brainpower, causes strong peristalsis (bowel movements), relaxes menstrual cramping, relaxes muscles, increases flexibility, helps build strong bones and increases alkalinity. Magnesium, as a primary alkaline mineral, opens up over 300 different detoxification and elimination pathways.

Heart Support

Dr. Bernard Jensen's research on the heart indicates that this organ requires two minerals more than any other, magnesium and potassium. Cacao, of course, is a fantastic food source of heart-supporting magnesium.

Magnesium is concentrated eighteen times greater in the heart muscle than in the bloodstream. Magnesium is the primary mineral missing when heart problems occur. Magnesium increases the overall vigour of the heart muscle. This mineral also decreases blood coagulation thus lowering blood pressure and helping the heart pump more effectively. An abundance of magnesium is effective in decreasing angina pain and in lowering some types of high blood pressure.

Chocolate to the Mayans and Aztecs was referred to as *yollotl eztli* (heart blood). Chocolate, as we know it, is known for its sensual love vibration. Chocolates are always given as love offerings. Interestingly, the magnesium levels and antioxidants in cacao support the heart directly. We have often heard that "chocolate opens the heart" — which is actually true.

Our personal experience of this has been profound. We feel that chocolate is helping usher in the "Cardiozoic Age" — the Age of Heart. Cacao seems to help correct the imbalance between mind and heart, allowing the mind to serve the heart. Increasing the heart energy brings forth compassion, wonder, healing and, most importantly, unconditional love.

Magnesium activates almost all the key enzymes needed for our neurons to produce energy from glucose, in the form of ATP (adenosine triphosphate) molecules. Magnesium is also necessary for the stable storage of ATP, so it will not spontaneously break down and waste its energy as heat. Proper brain function depends on a constant supply of ATP. When magnesium is in abundance then the brain works with clarity and focus. When magnesium is chronically deficient or depleted, then brain metabolism and brainpower are sharply reduced. Now we see why cacao is such an extraordinary brain food.

In the cerebrospinal fluid that bathes the brain and spinal cord, magnesium is present in higher concentrations than in the blood plasma. Of the 300+ different enzymes in the human body that require magnesium to function, a great many are crucial to cerebral metabolism and cognitive function. For example, magnesium activates glutamine synthetase, an enzyme responsible for converting waste ammonia — an extremely toxic byproduct of normal protein metabolism — into urea for proper disposal. The ability to focus and pay attention can be compromised by even small increases in brain ammonia.

Magnesium is also needed to activate the enzyme (D6D) that converts medium-chain omega 3 fatty acids (such as hemp seed and flaxseed oil) into DHA, the most abundant fatty acid in brain cell membranes. Deficiencies in DHA have been associated with numerous neurological disorders from attention-deficit disorder (ADD and ADHD), poor memory, post-partum depression and Alzheimer's disease.

Our brain needs magnesium to build the protective myelin sheaths that insulate the nerve fibers that network our nervous system.

Biochemist James South, an expert on brain nutrition, sees a remarkable similarity between the symptoms of attention-deficit disorder (ADD) and the symptoms of chronic magnesium deficiency. These include difficulty concentrating and remembering, confusion and disorientation, irritability and apathy, as well as muscular restlessness.

Magnesium and vitamin B deficiencies cause a reduction in the production of dopamine. Studies in animals have shown that a magnesium deficiency causes a depletion of brain dopamine without affecting brain serotonin and norepinephrine (noradrenalin). Active vitamin B6, by the way, increases the cellular absorption of magnesium and therefore works in concert to increase the production of dopamine. Natural active vitamin B6 (found in high concentrations in spir-

Le Cacao

Charles Plumier, *Cacao*,
from a manuscript on plants and civilizations in the Antilles, c. 1686

ulina, goji berries and bee pollen) increases the cellular absorption of magnesium and therefore works in concert to increase the production of dopamine. We will revisit the incredible synergy between spirulina, goji berries and bee pollen with cacao in the **Chocolate Alchemy** section of this book.

Magnesium is essential to the pituitary gland. This gland takes information from the hypothalamus in the brain and transmits it through the body as chemical messengers or hormones. These hormones directly influence the production of many other vital hormones in the body. Cacao's high magnesium levels thus have a marvellous effect in supporting balanced hormone levels.

When the pituitary lacks magnesium, it causes the adrenal glands to overproduce, thus increasing the heart rate, causing excitability and an inability to cope comfortably with daily challenges. This lack of magnesium leads inevitably to psychological, social, physical, emotional, mental and spiritual stress.

A Natural Laxative

Magnesium is also the primary reason why cacao works great as a laxative. Think about it, the major problem with Western civilisation is not war, the economy or crime; these are symptoms of a bigger problem — constipation! And cacao ends constipation! Imagine if everyone in Washington DC ate cacao! Can you see what this means for the future of the planet?

Soothing Menstruation

Accounts of chocolate causing PMS are unfounded and scientifically unproven. In fact, chocolate seems to soothe PMS symptoms as most women know intuitively. Woman have a chocolate center in their brain which informs them of the truth, while men tend to remain clueless. Low magnesium levels are likely the primary reason women crave chocolate before, during and/or after the menstrual period. Magnesium requirements may increase before, during and/or after the menstrual cycle. Other secondary reasons why chocolate cravings increase may be due to cacao's hormone balancing effects and its natural endorphins (anandamide).

Muscle Relaxation

To relax, muscles need magnesium. Magnesium increases flexibility and strength. A chronic magnesium deficiency leads to excessive muscle tension, including spasms, twitches and restlessness. This can be especially true of the hands and feet and facial muscles.

Bone Building

According to Professor L. Kervran in his book, **Biological Transmutations**, magnesium can be biologically transmutated into calcium. However, the reverse has not been observed. This accounts for the observation that increased magnesium intake has been shown to strengthen bones. It also accounts for the strange alkaline properties of high magnesium foods.

The Menier chocolate factory near Paris, France circa 1900

Signs of Magnesium Deficiency

- aggressive behaviour
- alcoholism
- amyotrophic lateral sclerosis
- anorexia
- apathy
- arrhythmia
- asthma
- attention deficit disorder (ADD and ADHD)
- blood vessel clots
- calcification of organs, tissue, and small arteries
- cancer
- cerebral palsy
- chronic fatigue syndrome
- cluster headaches
- confusion
- constipation
- convulsions
- cramps
- depression
- diabetes
- disorientation
- failure to grow
- fibromyalgia
- fluoride toxicity
- head injuries
- heart-related conditions
- headaches
- HIV
- hyperacidity
- hypertension
- insomnia
- irritability
- kidney stones
- migraines
- multiple sclerosis (MS)
- muscular weakness
- muscle tremors
- muscle tics
- myocardial infarction
- nervousness
- neuromuscular problems
- osteoporosis
- premenstrual syndrome (PMS)
- psychiatric disorders
- rheumatoid arthritis
- sickle cell anaemia
- stress
- toxic shock syndrome
- vertigo

Drugs That Cause a Loss of Body Magnesium

- Alcohol
- Alcohol-withdrawal-stress
- Cocaine
- Beta-adrenergic agonists (for asthma)
- Corticosteroids (CS) (for asthma)
- Theophylline (isolated for asthma)
- Diuretics
- Thiazide
- Caffeine (coffee)
- Phosphates (found in soda drinks)
- Nicotine

Other Causes of a Loss of Magnesium

- Physical or mental stress
- Excessive dietary fat - especially meats, nuts, and seeds
- High quantities of dietary fiber
- High quantities of dietary calcium
- Deficiencies of copper, boron, or vitamin B6

Research indicates that cacao contains therapeutic levels of magnesium. Therapeutic levels indicate an ability to reverse a deficiency as the following study indicates:

"Ability of a Cocoa Product to Correct Chronic Magnesium (Mg) Deficiency In Rats" by Planells E., Rivero M., Mataix J., Llopis J., Department of Physiology, School of Pharmacy, Institute of Nutrition and Food Technology, University of Granada, Spain. **Int J Vitam Nutr Res** 1999 Jan; 69(1):52-60

Abstract

Epidemiological studies have reported that Western diets are often deficient in magnesium (Mg). We investigated the ability of a cocoa-derived product, used in some European countries as a dietary complement added to milk, to aid recovery from chronic Mg deficiency in rats. The animals were divided into three groups, each of which received a different amount of dietary Mg. Rats in the Mg-deficient (D) group received an Mg-deficient diet (0.225 g Mg/kg food) during 8 weeks. In the cocoa-supplement group (D + CC), the rats consumed the Mg-deficient diet for 5 weeks, and were then switched for 3 further weeks to the same diet supplemented with 3% (wt/wt) cocoa product, so that the Mg content of the diet was 0.27 g/kg food. Rats in the control group (C) were given the same diet as in group D, except that the amount of Mg was 0.56 g Mg/kg food. We measured the concentration of Mg, Ca and P from ten rats in plasma, whole blood, skeletal muscle, heart, kidney and femur in rats that were fed the diets for 35, 42, 49 or 56 days. In animals fed the cocoa-supplemented diet (D + CC) significant improvements were found between days 35 and 56 in the alterations in Mg, Ca and P caused by Mg deficiency in all tissues studied. On day 56, kidney and bone concentrations of Mg and Ca had returned to normal. Our findings show that the habitual use of the cocoa product as a dietary supplement favours correction of the negative effects of long-term feeding with a diet moderately deficient in Mg.

Antioxidants

According to research cited in **The New York Times**, fresh cacao beans are super-rich in antioxidant flavonols. Cacao beans contain 10,000 milligrams (10 grams) per 100 grams of flavonol antioxidants. This is a whopping 10% antioxidant concentration level! This makes cacao one of the richest sources of antioxidants of any food. Compare the cacao bean to processed cocoa powder and chocolates which range in flavonol content from the more common concentration of 500 milligrams per 100 grams in normal chocolate bars to 5,000 milligrams in Mars Corporation's special *Cocoapro* cocoa powder.

Research has demonstrated that the antioxidants in cacao are highly stable and easily available to human metabolism.

Cornell University food scientists found that cocoa powder has nearly twice the antioxidants of red wine and up to three times what is found in green tea.

Their findings were published in an article entitled "Cocoa Has More Phenolic Phytochemicals and a Higher Antioxidant Capacity than Teas and Red Wine" found in the American Chemical Society's **Journal of Agriculture and Food Chemistry**, a peer-reviewed publication.

Scientists have known that cocoa contains significant antioxidants, but no one knew just how rich they were compared with those in red wine and green tea.

The Cornell researchers, led by Chang Y. Lee, chairman of the Department of Food Science and Technology at Cornell University's New York State Agricultural Experiment Station in Geneva, N.Y., say the reason that cocoa leads the other drinks is its high content of antioxidant compounds called phenolic phytochemicals, or flavonoids. They discovered 611 milligrams of the phenolic compound gallic acid equivalents (GAE) and 564 milligrams of the flavonoid epicatechin equivalents (ECE) in a single serving of cocoa. Examining a glass of red wine, the researchers found 340 milligrams of GAE and 163 milligrams of ECE. In a cup of green tea, they found 165 milligrams of GAE and 47 milligrams of ECE.

Lee and his colleagues used two chemical tests that measured how well the cocoa antioxidant compounds scavenge and clean up free radicals. Free radicals are renegade oxygen molecules that have been associated with DNA damage, premature aging, heart disease and cancer.

"If I had made a prediction before conducting the tests, I would have picked green tea as having the most antioxidant activity," said Lee. "When we compared one serving of each beverage, the cocoa turned out to be the highest in antioxidant activity, and that was surprising to me." Phenolic compounds protect plants against insects and pathogens, and they remain active even after food processing. A decade ago "food scientists did not know that phenolics had an important role in human health," says Lee.

University of California at Davis research demonstrated that antioxidant levels in the blood rose exponentially for six hours after the subjects consumed semisweet chocolate. Antioxidants can reach target cells in as quickly as 30 minutes when cocoa is consumed as a beverage according to studies done by Holt R.R., Lazarus S.A., Sullards M.C., et al.

A growing body of research has suggested that chocolate has beneficial effects on the cardiovascular system. **The Journal of Clinical Nutrition** and many other peer-reviewed publications have reported that the antioxidant polyphenols in chocolate are protective of the heart and circulatory system.

Research published in the **Journal of the American College of Nutrition** and the journal **Circulation** demonstrates that eating a few squares of dark chocolate daily increases the ability of the blood vessels to dilate. This study focused on flavonoids, another term for the antioxidants found in chocolate.

A group of eleven volunteers were given 46 grams (1.6 ounces) of dark chocolate rich in flavonoids daily for two weeks and compared with a control group of ten volunteers who were given dark chocolate low in flavonoids.

At the end of the trial, the researchers used ultrasound to measure how well blood vessels were able to relax if blood flow increased, a process called flow-mediated dilation. They examined the brachial artery in the arm; how well this artery dilates reflects the ability of the coronary arteries to dilate.

At the end of the two weeks, the arteries of the group that had eaten the flavonoid-rich chocolate had a greater capacity to expand, up from 10.2 percent to 11.5 percent, compared with a reduction in the control group. The senior researcher, Mary Engler, Professor of Physiological Nursing at the University of California, said: "Improvements in endothelial function — the ability of the artery to dilate — are indicative of improved vascular health and a lower risk for heart disease."

The researchers also found that concentrations of the cocoa flavonoid epicatechin, thought to be beneficial for blood vessel function, was higher in the high-flavonoid group. About this Engler added: "It is likely that the elevated blood levels of epicatechin triggered the release of active substances that vasodilate, or increase, blood flow in the artery."

The **Associated Press** reported, in August 2004, the findings of a study conducted by cardiologists at Athens Medical School in Greece indicating dark chocolate improves the functioning of the cells lining blood vessels. The study involved 17 healthy young volunteers who were given 3.5 ounces of either dark chocolate or fake chocolate. The study found that chocolate made the blood vessels more flexible thus decreasing the potential of hardening of the arteries and reducing the possibility of heart disease. Flavonoid antioxidants contained in chocolate were suspected of creating the noticeable improvement in cardiovascular health.

In other research, chocolate antioxidants have been shown to reduce the oxidation of low-density lipoproteins (LDL) or "bad cholesterol." Cocoa powder in an infusion concentration of 1.5% to 3.3% inhibits LDL oxidation as much or better than green tea. The oxidation of LDL is considered a major factor in the development of heart disease and strokes.

Additionally, stearic acid, the predominant saturated fat in chocolate, is a unique fatty acid which has a neutral effect on blood cholesterol levels.

Research recently carried out at King's College, London, suggests that chocolate antioxidants inhibit platelet aggregation (the clumping of red blood cells) which decreases the likelihood of atherosclerosis (degradation of the arteries).

Further research by the Department of Nutrition at the University of California at Davis found that not only does chocolate prevent platelet aggregation, it beneficially thins the blood as well. Thinner blood lowers blood pressure and decreases the possibility of blood clots or strokes. What was interesting was that their research demonstrated that the protective factors were specifically in the unadulterated cacao bean.

Studies done on the Kuna tribe of the San Blas Islands off of Panama by Dr. Norman K. Hollenberg, Professor of Medicine at Brigham and Women's Hospital and Harvard Medical School, found a connection between eating cacao and circulatory system health. Dr. Hollenberg found that the Kuna tribespeople had a high-salt diet, yet normal blood pressure and they consume locally-grown cacao at every meal. His study followed some of the Kuna people as they migrated into the city, where they started consuming commercially ground cocoa which caused their blood pressure to rise.

A study financed by National Institute of Health grants and Mars Corporation involved 27 healthy people ranging in age from 18 to 72. Each consumed a cocoa powder beverage containing 900 milligrams of flavonol antioxidants daily for five days. Using a finger cuff, blood flow was measured on day one and day five of the study. Researchers found a "significant improvement" in blood flow and in the function of the endothelial cells that line the blood vessels.

Research has recently been conducted on the effects of chocolate antioxidants on cancer. Cocoa powder has shown an inhibitory effect on human colonic adenocarcinoma in vitro.

In vitro studies have demonstrated the inhibitory effect of epicatechin antioxidants on human 5-lipoxygenase which may contribute to the reported anti-inflammatory effects of chocolate.

On top of, and in addition to all of this, a study of 8,000 male Harvard graduates showed that chocolate-lovers lived longer than abstainers. Their longevity may be explained by the high polyphenol levels in chocolate.

What all this is saying is that cacao is miraculous. Premium chocolate is good for you. Cocoa is at least as good and actually much better for you than red wine or green tea, and chocolate can actually save the planet.

Antioxidant ORAC levels per 100 grams

dark chocolate	13,120	strawberries	1,540
milk chocolate	6,740	spinach	1,260
prunes	5,770	raspberries	1,220
raisins	2,830	brussel sprouts	980
blueberries	2,400	plums	949
blackberries	2,036	alfalfa sprouts	930
kale	1,770	broccoli	890

Source: US Department of Agriculture / **Journal of the American Chemical Society**

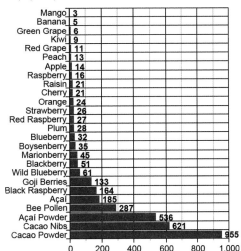

ORAC (FL) Comparison - Fresh Fruits

ORAC Value (umole TE/g)

Fruit	ORAC Value
Mango	3
Banana	5
Green Grape	6
Kiwi	9
Red Grape	11
Peach	13
Apple	14
Raspberry	16
Raisin	21
Cherry	21
Orange	24
Strawberry	26
Red Raspberry	27
Plum	28
Blueberry	32
Boysenberry	35
Marionberry	45
Blackberry	51
Wild Blueberry	61
Goji Berries	133
Black Raspberry	164
Açaí	185
Bee Pollen	287
Açaí Powder	536
Cacao Nibs	621
Cacao Powder	955

Brunswick Laboratories Wareham MA USA

Dairy Products and Antioxidants

Cacao and dark chocolate boost antioxidants; however, the addition of dairy milk cancels out the effects of antioxidants. Studies indicate that dairy products specifically block the absorption of all the great antioxidants in chocolate! Consider the following studies:

"Plasma Antioxidants From Chocolate" Mauro Serafini*, Rossana Bugianesi*, Giuseppe Maiani*, Silvia Valtuena*, Simone De Santis* & Alan Crozier†

Abstract

There is some speculation that dietary flavonoids from chocolate, in particular epicatechin, may promote cardiovascular health as a result of direct antioxidant effects or through antithrombotic mechanisms. Here we show that consumption of plain, dark chocolate results in an increase in both the total antioxidant capacity and the epicatechin content of blood plasma, but that these effects are markedly reduced when the chocolate is consumed with milk or if milk is incorporated as milk chocolate. Our findings indicate that milk may interfere with the absorption of antioxidants from chocolate in vivo and may therefore negate the potential health benefits that can be derived from eating moderate amounts of dark chocolate.

"Nutrition: Milk and Absorption of Dietary Flavanols"
December 18, 2003
Nature 426, 788 (18 December 2003); doi:10.1038/426788a
Mauro Serafini* and Alan Crozier†

Abstract

Serafini et al. reply — Our results indicate that there is an increase in total antioxidant capacity (TAC) and epicatechin content of plasma in people who have consumed dark chocolate, and that these effects are reduced by the presence of milk.

* Antioxidant Research Laboratory, Unit of Human Nutrition, National Institute for Food and Nutrition Research, Via Ardeatina 546, 00178 Rome, Italy

† Plant Products and Human Nutrition Group, Graham Kerr Building, Division of Biochemistry and Molecular Biology, Institute of Biomedical and Life Sciences, University of Glasgow, Glasgow G12 8QQ

Allergies

A recent study showed that only one out of 500 people who thought they were allergic to chocolate actually tested positive. The idea that chocolate is a common allergen has been around for a long time, but recent evidence suggests an allergy to chocolate is quite rare. It is more often the case that the person is in fact allergic to pasteurized milk and dairy products. Pasteurized milk is the number one food that causes allergies.

Acne

Research by US Naval Academy concluded that there is no evidence that chocolate causes or exacerbates acne.

Acne is likely triggered by the refined sugars added to chocolates. Refined sugar can cause hypoglycemia, hormone fluctuations, moodiness and skin outbreaks.

We have actually seen individuals who do react and get acne even after they eat high-quality, organic, dairy-free, 70%+ cacao, cooked chocolate bars. However, these same individuals have no reaction to eating raw cacao, even in large amounts (20-40 cacao beans in a day).

Our perspective based on experience is that cooking cacao changes the chemical structure of cacao causing it to be more allergenic, although the allergens even in processed chocolate are very low.

Methylxanthines: Theobromine and Caffeine

"When one has drunk this beverage, one can travel all day without fatigue and without taking any nourishment." — Bernal Diaz del Castillo, a soldier in Cortes' army whose memoir, published many years after his journey, remains one of the most famous accounts of the conquest.

Cacao can increase one's energy substantially. Cacao does contain the stimulating methylxanthines: theobromine and caffeine. Although the quantities of these substances range from 1 to 2 percent of the whole cacao bean, the effects are felt.

In 18 commercial specimens of cacao, A. Eminger (**Forschungsberichte ber Lebensmittel**, 1896, p. 275; see also **Amer. Jour. Pharm.**, 1897, p.113) found theobromine to vary from 0.88 to 2.34 percent, caffeine from 0.05 to 0.36 percent.

We are just beginning to understand that there is a difference between raw theobromine and caffeine and cooked theobromine and caffeine. Certainly, more research needs to be done. Our experience indicates that the theobromine and caffeine compounds in their raw, uncooked form have milder effects.

Consider the research done in homeopathy, a branch of medical science. Experimental provings of chocolate by homeopaths indicate its stimulating effect when cooked, but not when eaten raw. One experiment conducted with a decoction of roasted ground cacao beans in boiling water produced an excitement of the nervous system similar to that caused by black coffee and an excited state of circulation, demonstrated by an accelerated pulse. Notably, when the same decoction was made with raw, unroasted beans neither effect was noticeable, leading the provers to conclude that the physiological changes were caused by aromatic substances released during roasting.

Theobromine

The base chemical theobromine $(C_7H_8N_4O_2)$ is sparsely distributed in the plant world, occurring in 19 species, most of them in the Sterculiaceae and Rubiaceae families. Theobromine was discovered in cacao seeds by Woskresensky in 1841. Some other popular theobromine containing substances include: coffee, tea (*Camellia sinensis*), the world-famous yerba maté drink (which has a dynamic interaction with cacao) and the kola nut, a close relative of cacao, which is famous as a constituent of soda drinks.

Yerba maté (*Ilex paraguariensis*) tea and cacao together create a stimulating beverage of varying strength depending on the quality of the yerba maté. Together, of course, the two substances increase the levels of xanthine alkaloids, including: theobromine, theophylline, matteine and caffeine as well.

Theobromine can form as a metabolite of caffeine. This means that if one ingests caffeine, then, after some time, theobromine will show up in the blood and in the urine. Though still habituating, theobromine is milder and has about a quarter of the stimulating power of its sister molecule caffeine.

Theobromine gently stimulates the central nervous system, relaxes smooth muscles and dilates blood vessels.

Theobromine is a more effective cough medicine than traditional remedies. Peter Barnes, Professor of Thoracic Medicine at Imperial College London and colleagues, gave ten healthy volunteers tablets containing either: theobromine (the equivalent of about two cups of cocoa), codeine (a common cough suppressant) or a placebo.

As part of a standard test for cough medicines, the volunteers each inhaled a gas containing a derivative of chili peppers that induces coughing.

Those given theobromine needed about one-third more of the gas to produce coughing than those who took codeine; and they experienced no side effects. Codeine was only slightly more effective than the placebo at preventing coughing and has side effects such as drowsiness and constipation.

Theobromine is also a mild diuretic (increases urination) and had been used as a medical drug in cases where a heart attack had resulted in an accumulation of body fluid.

Theobromine is a cardiac stimulant. This is a reason why it had been used to treat high blood pressure. One of the reasons why dogs should not eat cacao or chocolate is because this food can cause a cardiac arrest since dogs lack the enzymes necessary to metabolise quantities of theobromine in excess of 100-150 mg per kilogram of the dog's body weight.

In humans, theobromine has quite long-lasting effects. Liver enzymes decrease theobromine levels by only 50% between six to ten hours after consumption.

It seems that theobromine is formed in the cacao seed and in its papery skin when it begins to sprout as a protective mechanism against bacteria. Theobromine has demonstrated cariostatic effects (it destroys the bacteria that cause tooth decay). According to Park, C.E. et al. (1979), cacao powder has proven effective to inhibit the growth of 102 types of bacteria. At least one antibiotic chemical responsible for this activity is theobromine.

According to E. Knebel (1892), the presence of a red hue in some fermented cacao beans is due to the decomposition of a sugar-compound in cacao under the influence of fermentation which results in dextrose and cacao-red theobromine.

Based on the evidence, we are lead to the conclusion that fresh (unsprouted) cacao seeds taken directly from the fruit contain low or no theobromine and therefore have less stimulating and habituating properties.

Caffeine

Estimates of how much caffeine is present in cacao differ, depending on the source. Consider the following estimates we came across in our research:

- A 1.4 ounce serving of chocolate contains the same amount of caffeine as one cup of decaffeinated coffee.

- A cup of hot chocolate usually contains about four or five milligrams of caffeine, which is about one-twentieth that of a cup of regular coffee.

- According to the Chocolate Information Centre, a 50-gram piece of dark chocolate — about the size of your average chocolate bar — will yield between 10 and 60 milligrams of caffeine, while an average five-ounce cup of coffee can yield up to 175 milligrams.

- 800 grams of milk chocolate contains the equivalent amount of caffeine present in a cup of coffee.

- One ounce of Hershey's Baking Chocolate, Special Dark and Milk Chocolate contain 26, 22 and 5 milligrams of caffeine respectively.

- A cup of coffee may contain 50 to 175 milligrams of caffeine, a cup of tea contains 25 to 100 milligrams, and a cup of cocoa beverage contains 25 milligrams to none.

Some believe that cacao generally contains no caffeine at all. This idea is based on the confusion between the sister alkaloids: caffeine and theobromine. The two stimulants are related and have similar structures, but are nonetheless different chemicals with different effects and properties.

The Biochemist, (Apr/May 1993, p 15) did chemical composition tests where they specifically distinguished between caffeine and theobromine. They typically found up to 1.3%, by weight, theobromine in chocolate. They also found other pharmacologically active compounds including up to 2.20% phenylethylamine, up to 1.54% telemethylhistamine, and occasionally up to 5.82% serotonin. They could not detect any caffeine at all. **The Merck Index**, 12th Edition, says that a very small amount of caffeine is found in the shell/skin of the cacao bean, but then the shell/skin are typically discarded before eating or processing.

We have seen that those who are caffeine-sensitive (have caffeine allergies) may react to processed chocolate with a strong headache or other symptoms and to cacao with a slight headache or other symptoms. This reaction could be caused by caffeine or theobromine. If this happens, we recommend immediately drinking a glass of water containing two tablespoons of MSM (methyl-sulphonyl-methane) powdered crystals, which typically alleviates minor symptoms of food-based allergies. Also, consider that dehydration is a causative agent in headaches.

In a study by Moffett A.M., et al., involving 25 subjects selected because they believed that eating chocolate caused their headaches, only two subjects consistently developed migraine headaches after exposure to chocolate (the subjects were given identical-looking bars which may or may not have contained chocolate). In a total of 80 exposures to chocolate, only 13 headaches were reported. Moffett, et al. summarized their experiment with the conclusion: "chocolate on its own is rarely a precipitant of migraine."

Research indicates that overdoses of chocolate in a range sufficient to deliver 300 mg of caffeine and 300 mg of theobromine can irritate the stomach and central nervous system.

Our experience indicates that eating raw cacao, over time, can actually desensitize one to the cooked xanthine components of processed chocolate. We have noted that individuals who would feel headaches or irritations in their breasts from processed chocolate, will feel improvements in these sensations by eating raw cacao over time.

Phenylethylamine (PEA)

Phenylethylamine (PEA) has been dubbed the "love chemical." Based on the hard, scientific evidence this is probably not true, but it sounds great! PEA seems to help create feelings of attraction, excitement and euphoria. When we fall in love our PEA levels increase and we become peppy and full of optimism. PEA is noticeably abundant in the brains of happy people.

The brain releases PEA when we are sexually aroused. PEA levels can peak during orgasm.

If we believe that things have gone wrong in our life however, especially our love life, our PEA levels drop. Those suffering from depression have noticeably lower PEA levels. According to the research, orally administered PEA has been noted to reverse depression symptoms in 60% of the patients tested with no side effects, chemical dependancy or tolerance limits over time (e.g. doses stay the same over time).

In 1982, chocolate was found to contain up to 2.2% phenylethylamine (PEA). Anecdotal evidence indicates that PEA is somehow related to chocolate's explicit effects as the pharmaceutical drug selegiline (l-deprenyl), which delays the breakdown of PEA, can accentuate chocolate's effects.

Chocolate seems to keep our PEA levels high, no matter what is happening in our love life. This is one of the leading theories as to why chocolate has the reputation of replacing lost love.

From a grounded, scientific perspective, PEA is the structural molecule behind catecholamine neurotransmitters such as dopamine, epinephrine (adrenaline) and norepinephrine (noradrenaline).

PEA increases the activity of neurotransmitters (brain chemicals) in parts of the brain that control our ability to pay attention and stay alert. Elevated PEA levels occur when we are captivated by an attractive person, good book, movie or project; this happens specifically during those moments when we are so focused that we lose all track of time, food and the outside world.

When the brain is flooded with PEA, the presynaptic vesicles will pull in PEA in preference to the neurotransmitter dopamine. Dopamine is then blocked from being deactivated and dopamine levels rise. Elevated dopamine levels are associated with increasing mental concentration and a positive attitude.

PEA also increases the effectiveness of another neurotransmitter, norepinephrine (noradrenalin). Norepinephrine increases feelings of joy.

PEA is found pre-made and in great natural abundance in two wonderful raw foods: cacao and blue-green algae (especially the blue pigments of algae). These two foods can elevate the presence of PEA in our brain.

Blue-green algae works with cacao in creating a strong ability to focus, stay in the moment and pay attention even if we suffer from Attention Deficit Disorder (ADD). Also, these foods help us to be more absorbed in whatever person or project is before us and we suspect this is part of what makes these two foods fantastic natural appetite suppressants.

Anandamide (The Bliss Chemical)

A neurotransmitter called anandamide (n-arachidonoylethanolamine) was isolated in chocolate by neuroscientist Daniele Piomelli in 1996. Anandamide is an endogenous cannabinoid naturally found in the human brain. Anandamide is a type of lipid (oil) known as "the bliss chemical" because it is released while we are feeling great. In fact, anandamide is derived from the Sanskrit word "ananda" meaning bliss.

It has long been known that the brain contains a receptor site that can be filled by the tetrahydrocannabinol (THC) found in cannabis. A receptor site is a structure on the surface of a cell that can lock onto certain molecules, making it possible to carry a signal through the cell wall — a "lock-and-key" system. This is how cannabis makes us high.

The chemical our body produces that normally fills this THC receptor site is anandamide. This means that eating chocolate can get you high, not to the level of cannabis, but to a noticeable degree nonetheless.

The pharmacological effects of anandamide indicate that it may play an important part in the regulation of mood, memory, appetite and pain perception. It may act as the chief component in the control of cognition and emotion. Physiological experiments demonstrate that anandamide may be as important as the more well-known neurotransmitters, dopamine and serotonin.

High levels of anandamide were found in young men who ran or cycled at a moderate rate for about an hour, according to a study published in the journal **NeuroReport** by the Georgia Institute of Technology and the University of California, Irvine. Anandamide may be responsible for the euphoric feeling some people experience when they sometimes call

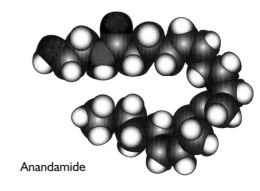

Anandamide

"runner's high." Arne Dietrich, the study's principal investigator believes the body releases cannabinoids to help cope with the prolonged stress and pain of moderate or intense exercise.

The findings of this study indicate that sufferers of glaucoma and cancer have alternatives to using cannabis for pain control and those are: exercise and... chocolate!

Anandamide Inhibitors

Not only does cacao contain anandamide, it also contains anandamide inhibitors. N-oleolethanolamine and N-linoleoylethanolamine, two structural cousins of anandamide present in chocolate, both inhibit the metabolism of anandamide. Essentially, these inhibitors decrease our bodies' ability to breakdown anandamide. This means that natural anandamide and/or cacao anandamide may stick around longer, making us feel good longer, when we eat cacao.

N-oleoylethanolamine and N-linoleoylethanolamine specifically target the endogenous cannabinoid system of the brain, mimicking the psychotropic effects caused by plant-derived cannabinoids either directly (by activating cannabinoid receptors) or indirectly (by increasing anandamide levels in the brain). To put it simply, these inhibitors promote and prolong the feeling of well-being that anandamide can induce or can amplify the effects of THC.

Neurotransmitter Modulating Agents

Because of cacao's large size we should call it a nut (like a cashew, which like cacao, is also the seed of a fruit). Normally nuts and seeds contain enzyme inhibitors that attempt to inhibit our digestion so that we do not eat the tree or plant into extinction. That is the main reason why eating too many raw nuts and seeds in a meal causes us to feel uncomfortably full, and also may cause constipation. With cacao, the situation seems to be a little bit different as cacao is a laxative and possesses other types of enzyme inhibitors.

From our knowledge of pharmacology, we believe that cacao contains no (or an insignificant amount of) digestive enzyme inhibitors, and instead possesses neurotransmitter modulating enzyme inhibitors such as monoamine oxidase enzyme inhibitors or related compounds (we already know, for example, that cacao has two anandamide uptake inhibitors, so it is reasonable to assume there are others).

Monoamine oxidase (MAO) refers to two classes of enzymes (MAO A and MAO B) that, in the human body, eat up or recycle neurotransmitters such as serotonin, dopamine, adrenalin, noradrenalin, etc. When we are young we produce lots of neurotransmitters and therefore experience more joy, curiosity and excitement. As we age, monoamine oxidase enzymes become more aggressive and recycle our neurotransmitters too early, therefore lowering the level of our neurotransmitters. A low level of neurotransmitters has been linked to depression, grumpy behavior, unpleasant moodiness and the process of aging itself.

Scientists, basing their work on ancient traditions of plant shamanism, have pursued the idea of using monoamine oxidase inhibitors (MAOIs) to inhibit monoamine oxidase enzymes (MAOs) thus allowing the level of neurotransmitters to increase.

Based on the study of certain plants an array of synthetic monoamine oxidase inhibiting (MAOI) drugs have been created by the pharmaceutical industry as antidepressants and youthening agents. However, according to the work of Dr. Gabriel Cousens and others, these synthetics have proven more erratic and dangerous than their natural counterparts. For example, synthetic MAOI drugs have proven dangerous when taken with processed chocolate (due to the presence of the tyramine formed in fermented cacao beans) and they should not be taken together. There is one major exception to the danger of synthetic MAOIs, a synthetic MAOI developed by accident by Dr. Ana Aslan of the National Geriatric Institute in Bucharest, Romania, has proven to possess youthening properties. This product is now widely available as an oral tablet called *Gerovital* or *GH3*.

Natural monoamine oxidase inhibitors called beta-carbolines (which inhibit MAO A) are found in the seeds of the Syrian rue plant (*Peganum harmala*), in the Ayahuasca vine (*Banisteriopsis caapi*), in Passion flowers (*Passiflora incarnata*) and in other plants. Natural MAOI's that inhibit MAO type B include nicotine. (The presence of nicotine as an MAO B may account for the unique phenomenon of certain organic tobacco smokers living long lives).

The effects of cacao as an antidepressant, as a youthening agent, an enhancer of intuition, an appetite suppressant and its ability to enhance entheogenic plants seem to place it in the same category as the other MAOI plants. We previously suspected, and now know, that cacao contains MAO inhibitors known as tetrahydro-beta-carbolines. Rumours that cacao is an MAOI—that once abounded in the world of chocolate alchemists—have now been confirmed.

Perhaps it is true that there is an energy surrounding cacao (immortalized forever in Roald Dahl's book **Charlie and the Chocolate Factory**) that creates beings who are inevitably transformed into zany, creative Oompa Loompas. Cacao does seem to make one younger. Remember the study of 8,000 male Harvard graduates who ate chocolate and outlived their peers.

Our experience from eating raw cacao regularly is that some pharmacological system is present in this food that heightens intuitive and psychic abilities. MAOI's are known to activate dormant parts of our brain and neurochemistry. This allows us to access some of the 90% of our brains we do not normally use.

Lose Weight, Eat Chocolate!

Anyone who eats chocolate knows that it diminishes appetite. There is evidence indicating MAOIs also diminish appetite.

There is actually no scientific evidence to implicate chocolate consumption with obesity. In fact, the reverse seems to be the case. Eating cacao helps one to lose weight. This is why nearly every weight-loss product on the market contains cocoa powder — which decreases appetite. Diet companies hint they are doing you a favor by providing chocolate weight-loss products, when in fact they use chocolate because it works!

Essentially, cacao makes one look, feel and behave younger, allows one to increase their psychic powers, as well as eat less and lose weight! No wonder the ancients called it "the food of the gods."

Tryptophan

Cacao contains significant quantities of the essential amino acid tryptophan which is yet another powerful mood-enhancing nutrient. From research obtained by cross referencing data on the internet, cocoa powder consists of somewhere between 0.2%-0.5% tryptophan.

The presence of tryptophan in the diet is critical for the production of serotonin, our primary neurotransmitter. Once in our bodies tryptophan reacts with vitamin B6 and vitamin B3 in the presence of magnesium to produce serotonin. Enhanced serotonin function typically diminishes anxiety and increases our ability to fend off stress. According to Dr. Gabriel Cousens, serotonin is literally our "stress-defence shield."

Tryptophan also helps produce other tryptamine neurotransmitters including melatonin and dimethyltryptamine, both associated with sleep. This may be a reason why the chocolate drink, even though high in stimulating theobromine with perhaps some caffeine is nevertheless more of an evening beverage than a morning beverage, as it typically does not cause insomnia.

Tryptophan is heat-volatile and susceptible to damage or destruction by cooking. As a result, tryptophan is usually deficient in many cooked-food diets, even if animal protein intake is high. (This may be a large reason why depression is on the rise). Eating cacao beans raw would thus be an excellent way to obtain dietary tryptophan.

Part III: Exotic Properties of Chocolate
The Meaning of Chocolate Insights

Las cosas claras y el chocolate
espeso. (Ideas should be clear
and chocolate thick.)
— Spanish proverb

Aphrodisia

"'Twill make Old women Young and Fresh;

Create New Motions of the Flesh,

And cause them long for you know what,

If they but taste of chocolate."

— James Wadsworth, **A Curious History of the Nature and Quality of Chocolate**

As with all languages, the peoples of pre-Columbian Central America often spoke in metaphors composed of words or phrases which, when uttered in sequence, had a hidden meaning. One of these metaphors was *yollotl eztli*, "heart blood" — their special name for chocolate.

Aphrodisia: a Chocolate Revival Party

Chocolate truly is food for the heart — it is the heart's "blood," due to its magnesium, antioxidants, love chemicals and esoteric properties.

Cacao opens the heart center. It heals not only on the physical, chemical level, but also on emotional, spiritual and metaphysical levels.

Chocolate is not fitted to be a medicine for just the heart however. Chocolate also possesses sensual, pleasureful and sexual energies embracing touch and fantasy. Some writers have claimed that 50% of women prefer chocolate to sex! Since the beginning of time, chocolate has been known as an aphrodisiac. Recall the legends of the Aztec Emperor Montezuma who purportedly drank 50 cups of hot chocolate before visiting his harem.

Dr. Henry Stubbe made chocolate for King Charles II. He doubled the normal amount of beans used. Dr. Stubbes was convinced, as were most of his contemporaries in England and Europe, that chocolate was an aphrodisiac. He wrote:

"The great Use of Chocolate in Venery, and for Supplying the Testicles with a Balsam, or a Sap, is so ingeniously made out by one of our learned Countrymen already, that I dare not presume to add any Thing after so accomplished a Pen; though I am of Opinion, that I might treat of the Subject without any Immodesty, or Offense. Gerson, the grave Roman Casuist, has writ *de Pollutione Nocturna*, and some have defended Fornication in the Popish Nunneries; hysterical Fits, hypochondriacal Melancholy, Love-Passions, consumptive Pinings away, and spermatical Fevers, being Instances of the Necessity hereof, natural Instincts pointing out the Cure. We cannot but admire the great Prudence of Moses, who severely prohibited that there should be no Whore among the Daughters of Israel, yet that most wise Legislator took great care for their timely Marriage; upon these very Accounts the Casuists defend the Protestant Clergy in their Marriages. And Adam is commanded in Paradise to increase and multiply, therefore I hope this little Excursion is pardonable, being so adequate to this Treatise of Chocolate: which, if Rachel had known, she would not have purchased Mandrakes for Jacob. If the amorous and martial Turk should ever taste it, he would despise his Opium. If the Grecians and Arabians had ever tried it, they would have thrown away their Wake-robins and Cuckow-pintles; and I do not doubt but you London Gentlemen, do value it above all your Cullisses and Jellies; your Anchovies, Bononia Sausages, your Cock and Lamb-stones, your Soys, your Ketchups and Caveares, your Cantharides (Spanish Fly), and your Whites of Eggs, are not to be compared to our rude Indian; therefore you must be very courteous and favourable to this little Pamphlet, which tells you most faithful Observations."

Casanova himself abandoned champagne in preference to chocolate.

Chocolate is one of the best natural sources of arginine, an amino acid. Arginine acts in a similar way to Viagra in that it increases blood flow to the penis and amplifies sexual desire.

Studies carried out by Alan Hirsch, the director of Chicago's Taste and Smell Research Foundation have shown that the mere scent of chocolate causes a slight increase in penile blood flow. Why or how is unknown.

In addition to the theobromine — which is also found in tea and coffee — chocolate also contains the previously-discussed, mood-enhancing neuro-transmitter phenylethylamine (PEA). Both theobromine and phenylethy-lamine stimulate dopamine production. Additionally, cacao itself contains dopamine. A study of mice and rats demonstrated that dopamine kick-starts a brain messenger chemical called DARP-32, which in turn activates hor-mones that make females more interested in sex.

Chocolate is, in essence, a gift to all lovers. It is an essential part of romance. Chocolate brings in the love vibration as many chocolate-lovers already know. A box of chocolates is the most celebrated gift for Valentine's Day.

Nobility

"Chocolate is a perfect food as wholesome as it is delicious, a beneficent restorer of exhausted power, but its quality must be good, and it must be carefully prepared. It is highly nourishing and easily digested, and it is fitted to repair wasted strength, preserve health, and prolong life. It agrees with dry temperaments and convalescents; with mothers who nurse their children; with those whose occupations oblige them to undergo severe mental strains; with public speakers, and with all those who give to work a portion of the time needed for sleep. It soothes both stomach and brain, and for this rea-son, as well as for others, it is the best friend of those engaged in literary pur-suits." — German chemist Baron von Liebig as quoted by the American Walter Baker & Company in the mid-nineteenth century, which like other chocolate manufacturers occasionally published pamphlets con-taining recipes and testimonials from nutrition experts.

The Spanish chronicler Sahagun's informants enlarged upon the unique noble qualities of cacao in the fol-lowing way:

"This saying was said of cacao, because it was precious; nowhere did it appear in times past. The common folk, the needy did not drink it. Hence it was said: 'The heart, the blood are to be feared.' And also it was said of it that it was (like) jimson weed; it was considered to be like the mushroom, for it made one drunk; it intoxicated one. If he who drank it were a common person, it was taken as a bad omen. And in past times only the ruler drank it, or a great warrior, or a commanding general. If perhaps two or three lived in wealth they drank it. Also it was hard to come by, they drank a limited amount of cacao, for it was not drunk unthinkingly."

Cacao imparts an ennobling energetic creativity upon the consumer allowing information to be downloaded from a higher dimensional space that surrounds us all the time. This creativity comes in a frequency that particularly suits the alchemist, astrologer, writer and orator. This property is esoteric, and may never be precisely pinned down. We believe the ennobling properties are carried in cacao's psychedelic purple oils which correspond to long-held lore that cacao butter contains the food's noble aspects. Monoatomic elements, which have an affinity for the oils of purple seeds in particular, may also play a role.

Notably, we find scholars always discussing and writing about the advanced state of Mayan mathematics and the uncanny precision of the Mayan calendar. We suggest the obvious, that both were inspired in the minds of chocolate addicts. It appears that the whole Mayan astrological phenomenon was downloaded from chocolate hyperspace!

Nature's Prozac (Anti-Depressant Properties of Cacao)

As we have noted, cacao is one of nature's richest sources of magnesium, the brain mineral. Cacao is also a great source of serotonin, dopamine and phenylethylamine, three well-studied neurotransmitters which help alleviate depression and are associated with feelings of well-being. Cacao contains nutrients and types of neurotransmitter modulating agents which allow serotonin and dopamine to remain in the bloodstream longer without being broken down. This increases feelings of well-being and helps one become younger. Cacao contains anandamide which delivers blissful feelings and anandamide inhibitors which keep the bliss chemical from being prematurely broken down. Cacao also contains a host of B vitamins which are associated with brain health. All this makes cacao a natural prozac!

Research by British psychologist, Dr. David Benton at the University of Wales in Swansea, found chocolate to be an excellent mood elevator. When he played sad music to a group of students, their moods sank. He then offered them the choice of milk chocolate or carob (a natural chocolate substitute that is similar in taste). Without their knowing which product they were eating, the participants found that the chocolate raised their moods, while the carob did nothing. Moreover, as their moods fell, their cravings for chocolate increased.

Cacao assists with the emotional creation of optimism, creativity, joy and child-like laughter. This is embodied in the Willy Wonka character: a zany, creative, absurd and optimistic alchemist from the book and movie **Charlie and The Chocolate Factory**. Willy Wonka is in essence a product of the spirit of chocolate itself!

Exotic Tobacco flowers from a farm near Mitla, Mexico

Tryptamines, Phenylalanines, Lactones and Cannabinoids

"The cocoa woods were another thing. They were like the woods of fairy tales, dark and shadowed and cool. The cocoa-pods, hanging by short stems, were like wax fruit in brilliant green and yellow and red and crimson and purple." — V.S. Naipaul, **The Middle Passage** (1981), Trinidadian author

"I, too, have experienced the mystique of old cacao plantings. There is something wonderful about a plantation of wizened old cacao trees. Within this

72

Mimosa tree at Monte Alban, Mexico

setting, moisture drips from every leaf and branch, and the mulch smells steamy and fresh. Little pools of sunlight filter through the large, flat leaves of the cacao trees, illuminating the leaf litter with its earth tones of russet, yellow, orange, and brown." — Allen M. Young, **The Chocolate Tree** (1994)

"The flowering chocolate drink is foaming,
The flower of tobacco is passed around.
If my heart would taste them,
My life would become inebriated."
— Tlaltecatzin, Aztec poet

Cacao has a long history of being used in combination with other psychoactive plants. Jonathan Ott, scientist and author of many books on entheogens, including **Pharmacotheon** and **Shamanic Snuffs**, has noted a strong correspondence between South American and Central American plant shamanism. Ayahuasca appears to be the key psychoactive medicinal beverage of indigenous South American Amazonian culture and mixed cacao drinks appear to be the key psychoactive medicinal beverage of indigenous Central American culture.

Cacao works to potentiate three primary psychoactive pathways: tryptophan/tryptamine, phenylalanine/phenylethylamine and cannabinoid/anandamide. Cacao works along other pathways as well. Evidence suggests that lactone compounds are also activated by cacao. Additionally, psychoactive plants that work on yet-to-be-understood principles seem to be enhanced by cacao. Again, although theorized for some time, it has now been proven that cacao contains MAO inhibitors known as tetrahydro-beta-carbolines that potentiate and positively flavor entheogenic compounds.

Cacao somehow enhances the absorption of and/or inhibits the breakdown of tryptamine alkaloids such as those found in magic mushrooms, morning glory seeds, baby Hawaiian woodrose seeds, iboga root, certain mimosa barks and flowers, as well as certain acacia barks. Therefore cacao can perpetuate and/or amplify the effects of tryptamine-based entheogens.

Magic Mushrooms

It is well documented that visually-stimulating, consciousness-expanding mushrooms were consumed along with cacao drinks in various Aztec and

Teonanacatl

Mayan rituals. The Aztecs called the magic mushroom: *teonanacatl*.

The best documented use of cacao and magic mushrooms together dates back to Aztec society. Cacao traders known as the *pochteca* (who were not actually Aztecs, but were the descendants of the Maya) would eat mushrooms in the evening and then continue boosting the effect with chocolate drinks all night.

The Spanish chronicler Sahagun wrote: "The first thing eaten at the gathering were certain black little mushrooms, which they called *nanacatl*, which inebriate and cause hallucinations, and even provoke lust. These they ate before dawn, and they also drank cacao before dawn." According to Jonathan Ott's research, another chronicler, Diego Duran, referring to a now-lost history text describing the coronation of Aztec emperor Ahuitzotl circa 1486 A.D., wrote: "In this whole story I have noted one thing: mention is never made that anyone drank wine of any kind to get drunk, but only woodland mushrooms which they ate raw, on which says the History, they were happy and rejoiced and went somewhat out of their heads, and of wine no mention is made...mention is only made of the abundance of chocolate that was being drunk in these solemnities."

Researchers Valentina P. Wasson and her husband R. Gordon Wasson found the traditional mushroom-cacao ritual still intact in Mexico. On June 29th, 1955, Gordon Wasson and a friend visited shamaness Maria Sabina in her home village of Huautla de Jimenez outside of Oaxaca, Mexico. On that fateful night Maria Sabina fed Gordon Wasson a cacao beverage with *teonanacatl*. In 1957, Wasson's experiences were published in an issue of *Life* magazine arousing the mass imagination of a new generation of Americans and helping to usher in the psychedelic era.

Swiss scientist Albert Hofmann's subsequent pioneering research demonstrated that the *teonanacatl* obtained for him by the Wassons contained the psychoactive tryptamine, *psilocybin*. Subsequent research revealed another active tryptamine in the mushroom called *psilocin*.

Why would one get the idea of adding cacao to mushrooms? As it seems to do with all entheogens, cacao tonifies or qualifies the effects of mushrooms. It adds a lightness and silliness to the effect, and decreases the probability of having a "bad trip." The spirit of cacao and the magic mushroom seem to be working together to expand consciousness and transform the planet from misery into hilariousness.

Traditionally in Mexico, mushrooms were crushed on a heated metate and then made into an aqueous infusion. This corresponds to today's general shamanic strategy of making magic mushroom tea (held for 15 minutes between 140 and 160 degrees Fahrenheit and not boiled) to deactivate the liver toxins generally found in all raw mushrooms. Multiple 15 minute extractions of the material may be needed to draw all the *psilocybin* into the tea water (squeezing the material at the end of each extraction helps draw the active principle into the tea). This tea can be mixed with herbs and then blended with cacao and other alchemical ingredients to create magic hot chocolate.

Up to this day, the shamans of Huautla de Jimenez still use cacao beans with magic mushrooms in ceremonies. Occasionally, in Western culture, chocolate treats will show up made with magic mushrooms.

Tree Barks, Flowers, and Dimethyltryptamine

The Leguminosae family contains a large group of pod-fruit bearing trees that often possess high concentrations of the mind-altering dream chemical *dimethyltryptamine*. Of these, it is likely that some types of Mimosa barks and

flowers were added to cacao potions. A plant in this group, probably *Calliandra anomala* (called *tlacoxochitl* by the ancients), similar to Bolivian calliandra (hair flower), grows in the Oaxaca region of Mexico. Researcher Jonathan Ott believes that twigs and flowers of this plant were added to cacao drinks.

South and Central American Virola trees (of which nutmeg is an Asiatic relative) possess the indole compound *5-methoxy-dimethyltryptamine* (5 MEO DMT) and thus visionary qualities.

A Mimosa flower

Virola guatemalensis bark is an ancient additive to cacao drinks. Interestingly, virola barks are also added to Ayahuasca brews.

Ayahuasca

Processed chocolate is not recommended to be used in conjunction with Ayahuasca (the tea combination of *Banisteriopsis caapi* vine and *Psychotria viridis* leaves), any of the Ayahuasca analogues (for example, Syrian rue seeds and Mimosa root bark tea) or with any pharmaceutical monoamine oxidase inhibiting drugs as it can lead to an adrenal and blood pressure reaction with the chemical tyramine found in the processed chocolate. As tyramine is a product of fermentation, fermented cacao contains measurable quantities of tyramine, yet, interestingly, unfermented cacao likely contains none. Further research needs to be done in this field.

le tiers de sa grandeur ordinaire.

Feuille de Cacoyer; d'environ

Cacaotier ou Cacoyer.

Cacti and Phenylethylamine

The phenylethylamine in cacao, perhaps in conjunction with unknown neurotransmitter modulating agents, seems to also help boost the effects of psychoactive New World cacti (San Pedro, Peyote) and other phenylethylamine/mescaline-based plants and substances.

Due to their natural synergy and presence in geographically nearby regions, cacao has been traditionally used with psychoactive cacti. Cactus shamans have been known to offer cacao (along with items such as feathers and eggs) to the spirit world as barter for the health of the ill. The Huichol people in present-day Mexico incorporate cacao as a sacred offering to the spirit world during healings and ceremonies; they leave cacao or chocolate where they cut peyote buttons from their root with the serrated edges of Joshua tree leaves.

Quararibea Funebris

For possibly thousands of years, the natives of the Oaxaca region of Mexico have added the dried aromatic flowers of *Quararibea funebris* to a chocolate concoction they call *tejate* that is used in the treatment of anxiety, fever and coughs.

The Linnaean category system gave to the species the name *"funebris"* as it was initially found by Western botanists growing in a graveyard.

Quararibea funebris flowers contain at least three lactone alkaloids: funebral, funebrine and funebradiol. These compounds possess subtle relaxing and mind-altering properties that are activated when added to cacao. Lactones, we might recall, gained the attention of Western science as the active ingredient in the Polynesian root Kava Kava with its numbing and relaxing effect.

Quararibea funebris grows into a giant tree that can feed several families indefinitely with its rich production of flowers. The tree was at one time widespread and growing wild throughout the Oaxaca region of Mexico where it is still available in the markets. Due to deforestation, it lost its once wide growth range. It can still be found in its wild habitat in Guatemala.

Quararibea funebris flowers in the Oaxaca market, Mexico

Author and researcher Jonathan Ott, following the lead given by mushroom expert Gordon Wasson, believes that *Quararibea funebris* is the previously-unidentified, entheogenic flower, *poyomatli*. If this is true, *Quararibea funebris* was known in the ancient tongue as *poyomatli, xochicacaohuatl* or *cacahuaxochitl*. These words literally mean, "flower of cacao" even though funebris flowers are not botanically related to cacao. In Mexico today these flowers are known in Spanish as "flor de cacao" or "rosita de cacao" or "madre cacao."

Cannabis

Strong consciousness-altering varieties of hemp cannabis were not likely to be found growing in Central America in pre-Columbian times. Even so, this plant deserves some elaboration as high doses of cacao seem to bring on a semblance of a cannabis high indicating a close affection between the two plants. Cacao is the only plant we know of, other than cannabis, to contain cannabinoids.

Cacao's anandamide (a cannabinoid) and anandamide inhibitors boost and potentiate the effects of cannabis and its major brain-active component, THC. The anandamide inhibitors theoretically block THC from being broken down thus amplifying its effects.

Cannabis in combination with cacao has physical medicinal effects. Evidence in the United Kingdom is beginning to accumulate on cannabis' herbal healing effects on multiple sclerosis. Now medicinal cannabis distributors have added chocolate to raw cannabis to potentiate healing. The mixture consists specifically of: cocoa powder, cane sugar, cocoa butter, lecithin, vanilla and 2% raw cannabis.

The 150 gram *Cannachoc* bars, as they are known, are made in volunteers' homes, with raw materials donated by well-wishers.

The distribution group calls itself Therapeutic Help from Cannabis for Multiple Sclerosis. Enquirers, who must provide a doctor's note to confirm their illness, may choose milk, dark, vegan or diabetic chocolate, and are recommended to take one piece three times a day to alleviate symptoms without causing a cannabis "high."

Similar medicinal concoctions can be made at home. To extract the fat-soluble cannabinoids, add raw cannabis (crushed by hand) to cold-pressed hempseed oil in the ratio of one gram of cannabis per one fluid ounce of hempseed oil. Leave this to extract at room temperature in a dark cupboard for one month; shake daily. To stay below the threshold of psychoactive cannabis effects, but yet still maintain medicinal properties, add only one or two tablespoons of this potentiated hempseed oil to your daily cacao beverage.

Cannabineae.

Cannabis sativa L.

W. Müller.

The mulberry tree is a relative of cannabis. These plants share the same Linnaean Order as Urticates. Eating the mulberry fruit, in its unripe state, is purported to have similar psychoactive effects to cannabis; this has not been scientifically proven. We have experimented with concoctions of fresh, organic, ripe mulberries in combination with cacao and have felt an amplification of silliness and absurd behaviour — but we could have just been having a lot of fun.

Salvia Divinorum, Datura, P. Auritum, Nutmeg, Magnolia and Marigold

Salvia divinorum is a psychoactive type of sage that has been spread by human hands in the mountain canyons near Oaxaca, Mexico. Cacao beans are traditionally left as an offering at each planting. A salvia tea made from the dry leaves mixes well with cacao. The effect of the tea is mild as *Salvia divinorum's* psychoactive principle, *salvinorin A* (a lipid diterpene) is deactivated in digestion and only activated by prolonged oral exposure (i.e. chewing without swallowing for 30 minutes) or through smoking.

Datura flower infusions were sometimes added to cacao drinks. Although extremely dangerous to ingest, datura possesses visionary qualities. The active chemical ingredient is the toxic compound *scopolamine.*

Piper auritum — a relative of kava kava (*Piper methysticum*) — is a traditional shamanic plant additive to the cacao drink. The "cord" flowers and leaves of this plant possess *safrole* and *isosafrole* in significant doses. These compounds are the precursors for making MDA and MDMA-type compounds. Most people now add nutmeg to cacao for a similar effect.

Nutmeg is a strong shamanic plant native to the Spice Islands near New Guinea in Asia. The nutmeg tree produces a plum-sized fruit with an orange-red skin containing a purple-brown seed (like cacao!). The seed is typically ground to form the nutmeg spice. Both the seed and skin contain entheogenic phenylpropene compounds (elemicin, myristicin, safrole).

Magnolia blossoms could be another psychoactive ingredient involved historically with cacao. Only specific types of magnolia blossoms would likely have any consciousness-altering effects. This effect is likely the result of nutmeg-like compounds that are possessed by magnolia.

Psychoactive marigold (a relative of the sunflower) was an important visionary substance traditionally added as an infusion to the cacao beverage. This variety of marigold's active principle is still not known. The Mayan (and Mexican name) for this flower is *cempazuchitl.* Known as the flower for the "Day of the Dead," it was an important herb in pre-Columbian times.

In summary, cacao seems to potentiate and positively flavour the effects of all entheogenic plant substances. The presence of cacao alters the experience to be more zany, hilarious and fun than normal. Cacao also boosts altered states of consciousness as they are fading.

Mural on the wall in the palace in Oaxaca, Mexico. It shows two shamans engaged in consuming a psychedelic beverage.

This is an artistic rendition of Pacal Votan's sarcophagus lid. Lord Pacal, also known as Votan, was ordered by the gods to go to America to found a culture. He became the Mayan preist-king, ruling the empire of Nah Chan Palenque (in present day Chiapas, Mexico) for 52 years.

This is the extraordinary lid of Pacal Votan's sarcophagus. Known as a Magician of Time, he understood mathematics as a type of language that transcended human verbal experience. He believed "All is number; God is a number; God is in All." Based on the visionary qualities of the lid, Pacal Votan was likely a cacao shaman of the highest order.

The Corn god and the Cacao god having a party

Chocolate As Medicine

"The persons who habitually take chocolate are those who enjoy the most equable and constant health and are least liable to a multitude of illnesses which spoil the enjoyment of life."
— A. Brillat-Savarin, **Physiologie de Gout**

Chocolate has a long history of being used as a medicine and with medicine. Here we recount some of the key moments in the history of chocolate as a healer since the arrival of the Spanish:

1528: The conquistador Hernando Cortez, who toppled Aztec civilisation in the sixteenth century, reported that *chocolatl* improved a person's resistance to disease and their stamina.

1529: Bernardino de Sahagun, the Spanish priest, arrived in Mexico where he was to remain and study for 61 years. He compiled oral histories of native informants in the most comprehensive text detailing Aztec culture ever published. The work was entitled: **Historia General de las Cosas de Nueva Espana** (General History of the Things of New Spain) sometimes called **The Florentine Codex**. He described various medicinal uses for cacao and included a warning against green cacao, which "makes one drunk, takes effect on one, makes one dizzy, confuses one, makes one sick, deranges one. When an ordinary amount is drunk, it gladdens one, Thus it is said: 'I take cacao. I wet my lips. I refresh myself.'"

1529: Agustin Farfan's **Tratado Breve de Medicina (Brief Treatise on Medicine)** listed the herbs of Mexico and their medicinal uses, noting that chocolate served as a hot beverage and is used as a laxative.

1662: In **The Indian Nectar, or A Discourse Concerning Chocolata**, the English explorer Dr. Henry Stubbe gave his preferred recipe for *Chocolata Royal* (mostly for pleasure) made with anise seeds, nutmeg, and cornmeal. Stubbe solicited his readers for anecdotes and other "preparations that I may not be ignorant of what effects Chocolata, or its particular ingredients have here in England... to inform or otherwise benefit men." He also noted that cacao can provoke "lustful desires" and that the addition of vanilla will strengthen the heart. He also notes the high fat content of cocoa and devotes much of his treatise to his experiments in attempting to remove the "oyl."

Dr. Henry Stubbes (or Stubbe or Stubbs who lived from 1632-1672) was perhaps the most widely respected and quoted English authority on chocolate. Dr Stubbes was a friend of the philosopher Thomas Hobbes (Hobbes became famous for his phrase: Knowledge is Power). Stubbes was said to have been a great chocolate alchemist. He believed that the cacao bean by itself was harmless, while most of the ingredients usually added to chocolate were harmful.

When he prepared chocolate for the great King Charles II, he doubled the usual quantity of cacao in relation to the other ingredients. Stubbes recommended that "cold" constitutions should add heating herbs such as allspice, cinnamon, nutmeg, and cloves to the concoction. Dr. Stubbes wrote of the aromatic Tuscan embellishments to chocolate including: musk, ambergris, citron and lemon peel.

Stubbes made the later popular claim that "one ounce of chocolate is equal in nourishment to one pound of beef."

1662: In the same year as the release of Stubbes' book, Cardinal Brancaccio of Rome decrees that drinking chocolate does not spoil a fast because it is a medicine for nearly every ill.

1704: The French food writer Louis Lemery wrote in the 1704 London edition of his 1702 book **Traite des Aliments** the following about chocolate: "It's strengthening, restorative, and apt to repair decayed Strength, and make People strong: It helps Digestion, allays the sharp Humours that fall upon the Lungs: It keeps down the Fumes of the Wine, promotes Venery, and resists the malignity of the Humours."

1719: In his **Natural History of Chocolate**, the Frenchman D. de Quelus recommended drinking chocolate for "exhausted spirits" and restated Dr. Stubbes insight that an ounce of chocolate "contains as much nourishment as a pound of beef." Quelus warned against its use by sedentary people. Quelus also provided recipes that broaden the applications of chocolate, such as mixing it with other substances, including powdered cinnamon for "a good purge."

French doctor, Herve Robert, published an extensive, medically-referenced book entitled **Les Vertus Therapeutiques du Chocolat (The Therapeutic Virtues of Chocolate)** in 1990. He concludes in his book that chocolate does not cause:

- Acne
- Migraines
- Obesity
- Tooth decay

Consider the corroborating words of Jonathan Ott in his book **The Cacahuatl Eater: Ruminations Of An Unabashed Chocolate Addict**: "Not only are cacao and chocolate products among the most nutritious foods known, but their consumption is not associated with obesity, tooth decay or acne, and allergies to cacao and chocolate are rare. Doctors, dentists and nutritionists, being unaware of the latest scientific research bearing on these topics, continue to toss out cautionary advice regarding consumption of cacao products, advice which is at best misleading, and at times just plain wrong. On the other hand, a subculture of health faddists or 'organophiles,' having taken this medical misinformation to heart (and thence to stomach), has embraced in the name of health and nutrition, substitute chocolate foods based on carob flour (powdered seed pod of *Ceratonia siliqua*), a product which is decidedly inferior nutritionally to cocoa powder. A veritable chocolate hysteria reigns, but it is all bosh, twaddle, balderdash, tosh, folderol, humbug, stuff and nonsense, 'mere smoke of opinion,' completely at odds with the facts."

Obesity is considered to be a major factor in mortality from heart disease, and chocolate is incorrectly perceived to weigh heavily as a cause of obesity. In research cited by Jonathan Ott, the researcher Brummer found no correlation between chocolate consumption and early death from heart disease after surveying statistics from 20 countries. Sugar consumption, however, was found to be correlated with this illness.

Chocolate does cause, primarily through the action of anandamide, anti-oxidants, magnesium, phenylethylamine, serotonin, theobromine, tryptophan and unknown neurotransmitter modulating agents the following:

• An increase of general health
• A lessening of depression
• A lessening of stress
• Enhancements of pleasure, including sex

In **The True History of Chocolate** by Sophie and Michael Coe, Philippe Dufour is cited, who wrote a book published in 1685 on chocolate. Dufour made a metabolic/medical distinction between cacao butter and the earthy cacao residues that is of special note. He said: "But this way I do in no wise approve of, for the fat separating it self from the earthy parts, this sinks to the bottom, and the other keeps on top, so that being thus drunk, the first (cacao butter) loosens the stomach, and takes away the appetite, and the latter causes melancholy."

In India, homeopathic preparations of cacao are used to combat hypotension (low blood pressure).

As with any food and medicine, remember that each will react differently in different people. We are biochemically and spiritually unique beings. Some people will know they have finally found the food of the gods, while others will remain indifferent. For some, cacao will be the great medicine they have always sought after, for others, cacao will be just another food.

In our experience, and after review of the literature and research, we have arrived at three conclusions about the medicinal value of cacao:

1) Cacao, like ginseng, is a potentiator (it amplifies the effect of medicinal substances taken with it). It is probably the ultimate alchemical delivery vehicle of medicinal substances into the human body.

2) And also, like ginseng, cacao has an enormous array of its own medicinal components such as anandamide, antioxidants, magnesium, phenylethylamine, serotonin, etc.

3) Unlike highly herbal ginseng, cacao is a tasty food that can be commonly eaten. Cacao crowds out the need for other foods. Cacao is an appetite suppressant allowing us to eat less and live more!

Consider the following research:

"Food of the Gods: Cure for Humanity? A Cultural History of the Medicinal and Ritual Use of Chocolate" by Dillinger TL, Barriga P., Escarcega S, Jimenez M., Salazar Lowe D., Grivetti L.E., Department of Nutrition, University of California, Davis CA 95616, USA, **J Nutr** 2000 Aug; 130 (8S Suppl): 2057S-72S

Abstract

The medicinal use of cacao, or chocolate, both as a primary remedy and as a vehicle to deliver other medicines, originated in the New World and diffused to Europe in the mid 1500s. These practices originated among the Olmec, Maya and Mexica (Aztec). The word cacao is derived from Olmec and the subsequent Mayan languages (kakaw); the chocolate-related term cacahuatl is Nahuatl (Aztec language), derived from Olmec/Mayan etymology. Early colonial era documents included instructions for the medicinal use of cacao. **The Badianus Codex** (1552) noted the use of cacao flowers to treat fatigue, whereas **The Florentine Codex** (1590) offered a prescription of cacao beans, maize and the herb *tlacoxochitl* (*Calliandra anomala*) to alleviate fever and panting of breath and to treat the faint of heart. Subsequent 16th to early 20th century manuscripts produced in Europe and New Spain revealed >100 medicinal uses for cacao/chocolate. Three consistent roles can be identified: 1) to treat emaciated patients to gain weight; 2) to stimulate nervous systems of apathetic, exhausted or feeble patients; and 3) to

Achitecture design from Mitla, Mexico

improve digestion and elimination where cacao/chocolate countered the effects of stagnant or weak stomachs, stimulated kidneys and improved bowel function. Additional medical complaints treated with chocolate/cacao have included anaemia, poor appetite, asthma, mental fatigue, poor breast milk production, consumption/tuberculosis, fever, multiple sclerosis, reduced longevity and poor sexual appetite/low virility. Chocolate paste was a medium used to administer drugs and to counter the taste of bitter pharmacological additives. In addition to cacao beans, preparations of cacao bark, oil (cacao butter), leaves and flowers have been used to treat burns, bowel dysfunction, cuts and skin irritations.

Chocolate And Pregnancy

Pregnant women rejoice! Finnish research indicates that eating chocolate is good for the baby. Scientists at the University of Helsinki, who asked 300 pregnant women to record their chocolate consumption and stress levels, found that daily chocolate treats had a positive impact on the unborn baby's behaviour.

Six months after the infants were born the mothers who had eaten chocolate reported more reactions such as smiling and laughter in their offspring.

"And the babies of stressed women who had regularly consumed chocolate showed less fear of new situations than babies of stressed women who had abstained," reported **New Scientist** magazine.

Katri Raikkanen and her colleagues who conducted the research speculate that the effects they observed could result from chemicals in chocolate associated with positive moods being passed on to the baby in the womb.

Nevertheless, high doses of chocolate (binge eating) should be avoided while pregnant based on research done on reproductive and developmental risks introduced by caffeine.

Chocolate Yoga

"The cocoa bean is a phenomenon, for nowhere else has nature concentrated such a wealth of valuable nourishment in so small a space." — Alexander von Humboldt, German scientist

Rudolf Steiner wrote that chocolate "tends to loosen the life body from the physical." We have found that cacao expands flexibility creating a feeling of festive relaxation.

One of our favourite past-times is to consume large quantities of cacao (between 20-60 beans per person) and then do one or two hours of yoga. The magnesium and the MAO inhibitors increase physical flexibility and the methylxanthine stimulants add several hours of additional power and strength.

Also, cacao drinks make it easier to live on a liquid diet. Without solid food, the digestive system relaxes and the entire body becomes more flexible. Any yogi who has experimented with fasting knows this truth: eat less and you become more flexible, capable and clear!

Overcoming Chocolate Addictions

The best strategy for overcoming chocolate addictions is to switch from processed chocolate to cacao. Cacao, being in its natural state, is less likely to be allergenic, addictive or reactive in the body. Cacao, of course, provides what all chocoholics love: the chocolate high without the hangover! Cacao alchemy is also a lot more fun!

Whatever you are going to eat, enjoy it. Letting go of guilt is a big step in overcoming any addiction. Consider that research at Northwestern University's Medical School indicates that the brain regions activated by eating chocolate when it is rewarding are quite different from those areas that are activated by eating chocolate when it is perceived as aversive (as a result of having eaten too much chocolate). The same could probably be said of many foods.

Among other ingredients, typical processed chocolate bars and cocoa mixtures contain phenylethylamine (PEA), magnesium, methylxanthines (theobromine, caffeine), fat and sugar. One of these ingredients is probably causing the craving. If you cannot figure out which it is, take the following supplements, beverages and/or foods to cover all five:

- Add 1,000-2,000 mg of the amino acid supplements DL-phenylalanine or L-phenylalanine along with 500-1,500 mg of tyrosine twice daily on an empty stomach (at least one hour before a meal). Start with smaller quantities and then increase.

- Drink eight to twelve ounces of fresh green vegetable juice daily. Green juice can consist of celery, cucumber, parsley, lemon with apple to sweeten. This juice is chlorophyll-rich and a great source of magnesium. Another idea is to add 600 mg of supplemental magnesium daily or 6 droppers full of liquid angstrom magnesium before food.

- Replace chocolate with theobromine- and matteine-containing yerba maté tea.

- Add two tablespoons of cold-pressed flaxseed or hempseed oil twice daily to your meals.

- Include the following supplement, sweeteners and foods recommended to curb sugar cravings (the amino acid glutamine, yacon root syrup, stevia and/or moderate levels of low-sugar fruits such as tart green apples, cucumbers, tomatoes, bell peppers, etc.).

- Include servings of superfoods in your diet each day for the brain-balancing amino acids and for vitamin B3 and B6. We recommend three handfuls of goji berries (sometimes called wolfberries), two tablespoons of spirulina, two tablespoons of blue-green algae and/or two table-spoons of bee pollen.

L-phenylalanine combines with tyrosine with the help of vitamin B6 to produce phenylethylamine which we find in chocolate. One study from 1986 showed that thirty-one of forty depressed patients with low levels of phenylethylamine responded well to large doses of L-phenylalanine (up to 14 g a day), making it an acceptable antidepressant (and an antidote for chocolate cravings).

"Chocolate: Food or Drug?" by Bruinsma K., Taren D.L.

Arizona Prevention Center, University of Arizona, College of Medicine, Tucson 85719, USA, **J Am Diet Assoc**, 1999 Oct; 99(10):1249-56

Abstract

Although addictive behaviour is generally associated with drug and alcohol abuse or compulsive sexual activity, chocolate may evoke similar psy-chopharmacologic and behavioural reactions in susceptible persons. A review of the literature on chocolate cravings indicates that the hedonic appeal of chocolate (fat, sugar, texture and aroma) is likely to be a predom-inant factor in such cravings. Other characteristics of chocolate, however, may be equally important contributors to the phenomena of chocolate crav-ings. Chocolate may be used by some as a form of self-medication for dietary deficiencies (e.g. magnesium) or to balance low levels of neurotrans-mitters involved in the regulation of mood, food intake and compulsive behaviours (e.g. serotonin and dopamine). Chocolate cravings are often episodic and fluctuate with hormonal changes just before and during the menses, which suggests a hormonal link and confirms the assumed gender-specific nature of chocolate cravings.

Chocolate contains several biologically active constituents (methylxanthines, biogenic amines and cannabinoid-like fatty acids), all of which potentially cause abnormal behaviours and psychological sensations that parallel those of other addictive substances. Most likely, a combination of chocolate's sen-sory characteristics, nutrient composition and psychoactive ingredients, compounded with monthly hormonal fluctuations and mood swings among women, will ultimately form the model of chocolate cravings. Dietetics pro-fessionals must be aware that chocolate cravings are real. The psychophar-macologic and chemosensory effects of chocolate must be considered when formulating recommendations for overall healthful eating and for treatment of nutritionally-related health issues.

These pyramids at Monte Alban, Mexico oversaw a culture based on cacao beans

Saving The Planet With Chocolate

"There was in those days a body of opinion which regarded tea and coffee as harmful and favoured cocoa. And I was convinced that one should eat only articles that sustained the body, I gave up tea and coffee as a rule and substituted cocoa." — Gandhi, **Experiments in Dietetics** (Chapter 17, p. 50-51)

Everybody knows what chocolate is. It has found its way into every corner of the globe.

Chocolate is the best food ever. It is the food of the gods. Chocolate is good and healthy for you. Pure cacao, of course, is the best ever.

Chocolate saves us from the ravages of pessimism by its truly ridiculous nature. Chocolate saves the planet through absurd comedy.

As all the ancient legends and teachings demonstrate to us, cacao has arrived to restore the balance between humankind and mother nature. When humans overcut the jungles and take more than is given, cacao teaches us to restore order and natural harmony.

Real chocolate chips (raw cacao nibs!)

Chocolate plays a crucial role in our collective destiny of saving the planet from the jaws of disaster at the last possible second in the greatest story ever told.

The complexity of the chocolate tree and its astonishing fruit and seeds reminds us that only a small portion of the tropical jungle's botanical and medicinal wealth has been tapped by human beings for practical applications. Great treasures await us if we can keep the jungle around long enough to investigate its mystery.

The tropical rainforests of the planet are threatened by greed. Loggers, miners and petroleum lackeys are all poised to pounce on our planet's most incredible resource. Since cacao enjoys the shade it can be planted directly in the jungle without having to chop down all the trees. It can be our primary buffer against tropical deforestation.

Cacao is an economically beneficial crop for local jungle villagers whose growth and harvesting provides financial incentives to keep the jungle canopy intact. The jungle canopy provides sanctuaries for birds, animals, and creates more oxygen. Additionally, planted cacao groves grown within the jungle do almost as well as wild cacao trees — they are less prone to disease and able to produce higher yields.

Cacao trees attract at least 80 different species of birds into jungle areas where they are planted thus increasing biodiversity. **Natural History** magazine in their report on "The Chocolate Tree" found that rustic cacao farms attracted and protected a greater variety of species (such as bats, canopy birds and migratory birds) than other types of agricultural lands.

Cacao trees are helpful nitrogen fixers (although not as significant as legume trees in the nitrogen-fixing department) and they contribute to the ecological system in which they live by driving nitrogen into the soil through their seasonal cycle. It now seems evident that cacao is an essential and integral part of its natural environment in ways that we have yet to recognise. In 1996, for example, a previously unknown species of bird — the pink-legged graveteiro (*Acronatornis fonsecai*) — was found living in the canopy above a cacao grove in Bahia, Brazil. Toucans seem to frequent cacao trees even though they cannot peck through cacao fruit skins and the short height of the cacao tree makes them susceptible to predators. Toucans seem to hang out in cacao trees just because they like them!

Because it is a nitrogen-fixer it makes all the other trees around it grow better. Avocado, breadfruit, coconut, mango, oil palms, orange, as well as medicinal trees (such as Neem) can be grown with cacao in a sustainable jungle environment.

Planting and growing cacao is a great way to save the jungles! Demand for organic (pesticide-free) cacao creates a viable economic enterprise in tropical nations already battered by social and ecological challenges. As of 2002, ninety percent of the cacao grown in the world was grown on small, 25-acre or smaller, farms.

Even when world cacao prices are low, a cacao farm can provide the household with food and generate income at local markets. If the farm is abandoned, the fruit trees will be reclaimed by the jungle and the habitat will remain conducive to preserving biodiversity.

Every year insect, viral and fungal diseases of cacao trees are increasing. Pesticide treatments seem only to complicate the entire dilemma and, in the long term, actually make matters worse. The chocolate industry estimates that from 35 to 40 percent of the cacao crop is lost each year to disease. Particularly in West Africa, there is a blight involving the capsid bug, which attacks leaves, pods, young shoots and roots. Crop damage by this insect appears so severe that a hard-hit area is said to have been "blasted."

Theobroma cacao is being stalked by three serious plant diseases — witch's broom, frosty pod rot (*Moniliophthora rorei*) and black pod rot (*Phytophthora spp.*) — all of which attack the pods and destroy the seeds and other parts of the tree.

Frosty pod rot can be somewhat controlled by removing infected pod-fruits. Witch's broom fungus, unlike frosty pod rot, seems nearly impossible to control. It forms tiny spore-producing mushrooms on parts of the cacao tree and these eventually destroy the beans inside the pods. Witch's broom has steadily attacked cacao trees in Brazil, where in just ten years, production of cocoa beans has dropped from 400,000 to 100,000 metric tons in spite of pesticide use. Interestingly, wild cacao trees in the rainforest do not seem to be as susceptible to the fungus.

In addition to the fact that pesticides do not safely protect crops, they are dangerous for our health as well. Lindane is a hormone disrupting pesticide (linked to breast cancer) that is sprayed on commercial chocolate crops in Africa. Lindane is considered toxic and an Austrian report in 1998 concluded that it is not possible to set a safe exposure level for lindane.

Lindane is due to be phased out in Europe following a European Union decision to ban it. Despite concerns about the health effects of eating lindane-contaminated chocolate and the risks to farmers using it, lindane is still being used in cacao-producing countries.

Supermarkets claim that levels of lindane in chocolate are going down, but they do not publish any test results, making it impossible for shoppers to know whether lindane is still showing up in their favourite chocolate. The last time that chocolate was tested by the British government three quarters of the samples contained residues of lindane and twenty out of twenty of food industry samples contained lindane.

Special Note: We have joined forces with an organization that has mastered an inexpensive 100% natural, pesticide-free technique that can help save cacao trees, increase yields and stop all cacao diseases, including witch's broom fungus, in their tracks. We are currently available to connect chocolate growers worldwide with this organization in order to stop this blight on the world's greatest food. If you deal with direct, large-scale cacao agriculture, and wish to stop cacao diseases naturally, please contact us at the web sites and e-mails listed at the back of this book.

Child Slavery

A foundation report states: "Small farmers are at the heart of sustainable cocoa growing. Today five to six million farmers, many of whom live in poverty, grow more than 85 percent of the world's cocoa. Each farmer generally owns two and a half to five acres of land and grows about 1,000 cocoa trees."

As much as 70 percent of the world's cacao crop today is grown in West Africa, which once provided slaves to harvest cacao in the New World. The Ivory Coast now leads the continent in producing cacao (and in fact is the world's largest supplier of cacao), but Ghana from about 1910 to 1970 produced more cacao beans than any other region.

With 600,000 cacao plantations, The Ivory Coast leads the world in cacao production. Due to the intensity of cacao production in that country, sinister methods have been employed to enslave children to work on commercial cacao farms. The BBC exposed this in a documentary aired in the year 2000. The multibillion dollar commercial American chocolate industry is controlled by giant candy conglomerates who use Ivory Coast cacao. Therefore, they are directly supporting child slavery. This is yet another reason to purchase certified organic cacao or chocolate.

The following report appeared in the English newspaper **The Express** as recently as September 27, 2000: "Chocolate, it seems, carries modern-day slavery into our homes." Documentary filmmakers Kate Blewett and Brian Woods had encountered slave conditions on cacao plantations in the Ivory Coast and produced a documentary called **Slavery**. Blewett and Woods had been honoured in 1998 with a Robert F. Kennedy Journalism Award for their film **Innocents Lost**, about children stolen from their homes in Bangladesh and elsewhere and taken to the United Arab Emirates to be used as camel jockeys. In preparing a new film about stolen Indian children, some of which were made to work as domestic servants in London and Washington DC, the filmmakers visited about one hundred small cacao farms in the Ivory Coast, where they also found children being exploited. "We wanted a way of bringing it home to people in the West and not letting it be something people could watch and go 'Isn't it terrible what people in far-off lands do to other people in far-off lands,'" Woods was quoted as saying in an article published in **The Guardian** on September 28, 2000.

As a result of the negative publicity, the "fair-trade" chocolate standard has become popular. Fair-trade chocolate indicates that cacao farmers are being paid fairly so that they can educate their children and pay their workers. The US Department of Agriculture, the US Agency for International Development, the United Nations Development Program, the Smithsonian Institutions, Conservation International, the British Cocoa and Chocolate

Association, the ACRI, and the French Cocoa Research Organisation say they are all working together to promote and advance sustainable fair-trade cocoa growing. All these organisations are essentially either large corporations or acting as agents of large corporations. Therefore they answer to financial interests first, instead of ethics and ecology. That means the best way we can influence their role is to create economic incentives for them by voting with our money. Essentially, our message to them is to create sustainable, organic cacao growing farms and make the organic, raw cacao beans available to everyone in the world through widespread distribution channels in order for us to purchase the original product, while compensating organic cacao farmers with reasonable prices and wages.

Cacao Farms of the Future

Our goal is to create demand for cacao farms that are healthy, canopy-respecting and organic, so that we can indeed save the planet with chocolate.

Continuing research into cacao cultivation indicates that it grows best and is most productive in or near its indigenous jungle environment. Small farms, of less than 50 acres, enclosed or enveloped in tropical jungle rain forest and grown with other diversified tropical tree crops produce optimal cacao fruit and seed. Pollination, under these conditions, is certainly higher as the midge species can reproduce in great enough quantities to do the job of cacao flower pollination.

A Final Thought

"If we could sniff or swallow something that would, for five or six hours each day, abolish our solitude as individuals, atone us with our fellows in a glowing exultation of affection and make life in all its aspects seem not only worth living, but divinely beautiful and significant, and if this heavenly, world-transfiguring drug were of such a kind that we could wake up [the] next morning with a clear head and an undamaged constitution — then, it seems to me, all our problems (and not merely the one small problem of discovering a novel pleasure) would be wholly solved and the earth would become paradise." — Aldous Huxley (1894-1963)

Part IV: Chocolate Alchemy

"Chocolate is a divine, celestial
drink, the sweat of the stars,
the vital seed, divine nectar, the
drink of the gods, panacea and
universal medicine."
— Geronimo Piperni

Curing by Contraries

Knowing the energies of different foods can help create a more balanced diet and cuisine.

An ancient healing principle popular through many traditions, including European folk herbalism, is called: "curing by contraries." This principle provides that "cooling" herbs and foods heal a "hot" fever. Foods are often classified by this principle. According to this method of classification, cacao is cooling.

As a general rule, the foods of civilisation (potato products, meats, breads, cheeses) are heating, and thus cooling foods, such as cucumbers, celery, or cacao have great value.

Foods may also be classified as wet or dry. Many raw foods are generally wet, such as fresh juices, salads, fruits, coconuts and others. Cacao, however, has a drying property. We have noticed through living on chocolate beverages without solid food for days at a time, that our bowel elimination cycles are solid, perfect and dry.

In terms of balancing the energy of cacao in your own chocolate alchemy, consider that cacao is considered to have a cooling, drying energy. It balances excessive heat in the body and dampness. This would mean that chocolate is good for a fever or for diarrhea. It also means that cacao has great synergy with heating and/or wet substances. Hence, we see the unique alchemy of cacao, cayenne and hot water in the ancient Mayan and Aztec beverage.

Foods also fall on the spectrum of female and male (yin and yang) energies — some herbs and plants have more male (yang) qualities, such as hot chilies, durian (exotic fruit) and ginseng (herb). And some have more female (yin) qualities, such as passion fruit, papaya and pau d'arco (herb). Cacao is male, but slightly effeminate (subtly yang), so it has slightly better synergy with female energies and female plants, but that tendency is slight.

If all that was not enough, we also find that if cacao is abused, a hidden subtle heating energy can begin to arise, shift the alchemical dynamics and cause headaches. This is probably the methylxanthines (theobromine and caffeine) accumulating in the liver and body. Abuses of cacao would include: eating too much cooked cacao (chocolate products), eating raw cacao every day without rest, and eating more than 60 cacao beans in a day. As with any food, one should observe cycles of consumption and rest.

Naked Chocolate

Due to its concentration of neurotransmitter modulating agents and unique chemistry, cacao itself has some powerful psychoactive, brain-enhancing properties. Our experience has been that cacao retains much stronger psychoactive properties when eaten "naked" — without blending or heating.

We know, for example, that contact with metal destroys as much as 50% of the vitamin C in fruits. A similar principle is at work here with the cacao (which, by the way, is extraordinarily high in vitamin C!). One or more of the psychoactive chemical compounds in cacao is diminished by exposure to metal (knives, blending). More cacao is required to get the same psychoactive effects if you blend or cut them with metal — instead of eating them naturally, plain, naked.

The loss of potency ratio seems to be that 5 naked cacao beans are equivalent to 12-15 blended cacao beans. This is entirely subjective. It is just a guess based on our experience and sensory acuity. Test and experiment with this yourself. You may find, as we have, that it is great to grind cacao down with a stone mortar and pestle before adding it to smoothies and drinks, that way you do not have to expose the cacao to too much blending.

Organic Food

We are both sold on the fact that organic food (grown without pesticides) is far superior to conventional food (chemical-grown food) in its taste, appearance, mineral-content and sustainability. We always recommend that you choose organic ingredients for all your culinary and dietary needs.

The Ancient Chocolate Drink

In the inscriptions of the Mayan glyphs, the word for cacao is often modified by adjectives such as "chili cacao" or "fruity cacao" indicating different common recipe combinations. The Aztecs probably inherited recipes for making cacao drinks from their Mayan predecessors. The basic technique was to grind raw cacao beans on a metate warmed by a small fire underneath. Hot water was added to turn the cacao into a paste. More hot water was added to the paste in a jug creating a bitter hot chocolate. Then the mixture was whipped with a wooden *molinillo* (The ancient *molinillo* was made out of the dried and cut tepihilote palm. By using both hands a rotary motion of the *molinillo* can be created. As the spinning *molinillo* is dipped into the chocolate drink it blends and whisks the ingredients — a natural blender!). The drink was finally poured from one jug-container to another until a frothy beverage was produced. This could be drunk straight or other ingredients could be added. Common ancient cacao drink additives included:

Aak (a type of grass used as a foaming agent)
Achiote (annatto seed, *Bixa orellana*)
Agave cactus nectar
Allspice (*Pimienta dioica*)
Cempoaxochitl (*Tagetes erecta*) (Cempazuchil, Cempasuchil, or Flor del Muerto; the flower for the Day of the Dead, a Mexican Marigold)
Eloxochitl (*Magnolia dealbata*)
Honey
Hot chilies (*Capsicum, spp.*)
Hueinacaztli or Teonacaztli or Xochinacaztli (an Annonaceae or Cherimoya family flower, *Cymbopetalum penduliflorum*)

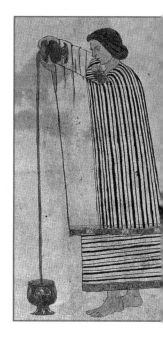

Itsim-te (*Clerodendrum ligustrinum*)
Izquixochitl, popcorn flower (*Bourreria, spp.*)
Maize (corn) or Nixtamalli (*Masa harina*) (corn flour treated with lime)
Mamey sapote (the heart of the sapote seed was often used, *Pouteria sapota*)
Olloxochitl or Heart flower (*Magnolia mexicana*)
Passion fruit (*Passiflora, spp.*)
Pochotl (seeds of the ceiba tree, *Ceiba pentandra*)
Quararibea funebris flowers (*Poyomatli*)
Spirulina
Suqir (a vine which acts as a foaming agent)
String flower (a relative of kava, *Piper sanctum*)
Vanilla (*Vanilla planifolia*)

The chocolate drink served in Montezuma's court was seasoned with chilies, achiote, vanilla and corn. The resulting drink, served cold, was spicy and usually bitter, although honey was occasionally used. When the Spanish arrived, they had mixed opinions about the drink, yet the practice of chocolate alchemy eventually won through. One Spanish soldier wrote that cacao "would be better thrown to the pigs than consumed by men." A recipe written down in 1631 by Spanish physician Antonio Colmenero records the following: "For every hundred cacao beans, mix two pods of chile or Mexican pepper ... or, failing those, two Indian peppercorns, a handful of aniseeds, two of those flowers known as 'little ears' or vinacaxtlides, and two of those known as mesasuchi ... Instead of the latter, one could include the powder of six roses of Alexandria, a little pod of logwood, two drachmas of cinnamon, a dozen almonds and as many hazelnuts, half a pound of sugar, and enough annatto to give colour to the whole."

Cacao's Best Friends

Cacao has a great affinity for certain plants. Of these, certain major plant friends that are on the inner family circle deserve further exploration:

Agave Cactus Nectar

One of cacao's best friends is the agave cactus (which we sometimes call the "century plant"). When the agave plant is mature, which takes anywhere from ten to twelve years, and begins shooting up a flowering stalk, the trunk of the stalk is cut, the stalk removed, and the base where the stalk had been is scooped out. Large quantities of hydrating, cooling, watery sap pour forth, and can be collected in bowls over a period of several weeks. This sap naturally ferments into a mild wine that the ancients called octli or pulque. Agave sap was often consumed with cacao in ancient Mexico City.

If the entire mature agave plant is dissolved with chemicals and enzymes and cooked, it can be turned into a sweetener known as agave syrup or agave nectar. The highest quality agave syrups are clear with slightly yellow overtones. If the entire mature agave plant is heat distilled into a hard alcohol, it is called tequila.

Bee Pollen

Cacao has great synergy with flowers in general and the pollen of flowers in particular. The Aztec Lord of the Flowers, *Xochipilli*, was the god most associated with cacao in that pantheon.

Bee pollen is the pollen produced by flowers that honey bees gather and bring back to the hive. Pollen grains are microscopic in size and bees collect millions of these individual grains and connect them with nectar into small pellets.

Bee pollen is an alkaline food considered by nutritionists to be the most complete food found in nature.

Bee pollen is a rich source of high-quality protein and contains all essential amino acids. Its high levels of protein and amino acids make it a great strength builder and brain food. Some of the amino acids present include: cystine, lysine, histidine, arginine, aspartic acid, threonine, glutamine, proline, glycine, alanine, valine, methionine, isoleucine, leucine, tyrosine, phenylalanine and tryptophan.

Some of the minerals found in bee pollen include: barium, boron, calcium, copper, iodine, iron, magnesium, manganese, phosphorus, potassium, selenium, sodium and zinc.

Bee pollen contains vitamins A, B, C and E. It is extraordinarily rich in most of the B vitamins, including folic acid (folate).

Bee pollen contains over 5,000 enzymes. The phytonutrients (such as co-enzymes, bioflavonoids, phytosterols and carotenoids) found in bee pollen also number in the thousands. Bee pollen is 15% natural lecithin.

Some of the benefits of bee pollen consumption include:
- Increases energy and stamina
- Increases muscle growth and definition
- Builds immune system
- Has antioxidant activity
- Enhances sexuality and fertility
- Smoothes wrinkles

Carob

Carob is an alkaline, legume fruit with a cacao-like taste. It is often used as a substitute for chocolate, but it just does not cut the mustard, if you know what we mean. Cacao has eight times as much protein, nine times as much fat, ten times as much phosphorus, over six times as much iron, twice as much potassium, twice as much riboflavin, fifty percent more niacin and only six percent more calories. However, when carob is used in conjunction with cacao, the real magic is revealed. The rich calcium content of carob combines alchemically with the rich magnesium content of cacao creating a most fantastic taste explosion.

Cashews

Cacao has great synergy with many nuts and seeds. Perhaps cacao's favourite nut is the cashew. The cashew, like cacao, is the seed of the fruit of an American jungle tree. The cashew, like cacao, is high in magnesium. Cashews are loved by many probably because they contain more sugars (carbohydrates) than other nuts.

If you find yourself looking for raw cashews, keep in mind that most cashews sold on the market, even if labelled "raw" are not actually raw! They have been heat steamed. Look for cashews that are certified as truly raw! We like the ones with their paper-like, creamy-tasting skins still intact.

Chilies (Cayenne and other Dried Hot Peppers)

Universally popular throughout Central America from ancient times to the present is the addition of spicy, hot peppers (*Capsicum annum*) to chocolate. Ground, dried chilies were part of the Mayan sacred drink. Ground, powdered chili pepper is now often called cayenne. The sulphur-rich components of hot peppers (cayenne) dilate capillaries allowing cacao and all its goodies to reach the cells more easily.

Cinnamon

Cinnamon is a tropical tree bark that originally comes from Asia. Cinnamon is a great source of the mineral chromium which helps balance blood sugar levels. If you sweeten your cacao drinks or treats we recommend that you use cinnamon to help balance the effects of the sugar on your bloodstream. Cinnamon has a spicy component which helps to dilate capillaries and deliver fat-soluble goodies found in cacao.

Cinnamon bark

Coconuts

All parts and derivate products of the coconut work wonderfully with cacao. Coconut and cacao love each other.

Coconut water is the breast milk of mother earth. Coconut water is the highest natural source of electrolytes. And this water is the perfect base for any cacao drink.

Coconut flesh is the "meat" on the inside of the coconut. In young coconuts this flesh is soft, in older coconuts this flesh is hard. In general, young coconuts with their "spoon meat" are much more fun than the hard, fibrous, tough mature coconut flesh. Young coconut flesh is a great rejuvenator of sexual energy. When young coconut flesh is blended with coconut water, the mixture is called coconut milk. Coconut milk is another great base for your cacao drink!

Coconut oil/butter is the oil from the mature, hard coconut flesh. Coconut oil contains antiviral, antimicrobial and antifungal properties. It has the highest level of energy of any oil and the least calories. It also requires the least amount of liver strength to digest.

Coconut oil is a fantastic builder of hormones — especially progesterone and testosterone.

Progesterone and testosterone tend to help increase biological levels of the feel-good neurotransmitters dopamine and serotonin.

We recommend coconut oil as a standard addition to any cacao drink or treat.

Coconut oil, as with any oil, should be cold-pressed and packaged in dark glass bottles (not plastic, as plastic can leach into coconut oil).

Honey

Honey is a universal medicine, sweetener and nutrient resource. A tremendous amount of research on honey has been done in Russia over the last hundred years. This research indicates: that honey is nature's richest source of healing enzymes and that honey increases reflexes, increases mental alertness and even increases IQ! Some types of Manuka honeys from the New Zealand rainforests have been shown to have antifungal, antibiotic and antiviral effects. All honey should be eaten raw, as cooked honey has no enzymes.

Honey is inappropriate for children under the age of one.

Maca

Maca is the great superfood coming out of Peru. Maca is a radish-like root, that is generally sold in its dried, powdered form.

Maca is found growing at elevations of over 10,500 feet in the Altiplano region of the Andes. Its natural zone is an inhospitable region of intense sunlight, violent winds and below freezing weather. With its extreme temperatures and poor rocky soil, the area rates amongst the world's worst farmland, yet over the centuries, maca flourishes under these conditions.

Maca has been used as an immunostimulant, for anaemia, to stop bone-mineral loss, enhance memory, fight stomach cancer, as well as to alleviate depression, menstrual disorders, menopause symptoms, sterility and other reproductive and sexual disorders.

Maca increases overall vigour — especially sexual stamina and appetite. All you have to do is dip a peeled cacao bean in agave nectar or honey and then dip it in maca powder. Once you do that, you will know the truth.

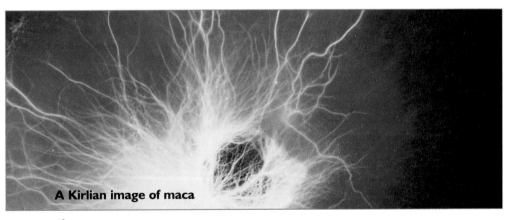

A Kirlian image of maca

Mint

Mint is the only green-leafy food that really generates magic with cacao. Working on a similar principle to cayenne, the menthols in mint dilate blood capillaries allowing cacao's magic to be delivered. Additionally, mint, being a green-leafy vegetable, contains high levels of calcium which synergise with the magnesium in cacao.

Peanut (Amazonian Jungle Peanut)

Have you ever wondered why peanuts and chocolate go so well together? Did you know that they have thousands of years of history of being mixed together in Amazonian shamanism? The Amazonian jungle peanut is perhaps the highest natural source of vitamin B3. Vitamin B3 (niacin) is an excellent cardiovascular dilator, just like the theobromine and theophylline found in cacao! The Amazonian jungle peanut and cacao, when mixed together, make for an outstanding delivery system for herbs and superfoods because they dilate our cardiovascular system allowing for nutrients and herbal medicines to get to our cells more easily.

The Amazonian jungle peanut is the world's original, ancient, toxin-free peanut. Bursting with flavor, these peanuts contain 40% oleic acid, 26% protein, all 8 essential amino acids, vitamin B2, B3, B6 and B9, vitamin E, and co-enzyme Q10.

Depending on growing conditions, jungle peanuts may contain boron, calcium, chromium, cobalt, copper, iron, magnesium, manganese, molybdenum, nickel, phosphorous, potassium, selenium, sodium and zinc.

Peanuts are a significant source of anti-aging resveratrol. This compound helps fight cardiovascular disease and lowers cancer risk.

Spirulina

Spirulina is the great protein-rich, superfood algae grown by the ancient Aztecs and still available to us today in health-food stores. Spirulina contains more protein than any other food on earth. The ancients ate it with cacao. We recommend that you try it too!

Vanilla

Vanilla is the only orchid fruit produced by more than 35,000 orchid varieties around the world. Orchids are the largest family of flowering plants in the world. Orchids are breatharian plants — this means they can survive just on air and ambient moisture alone. And vanilla is the fruit of this plant! No wonder vanilla is so incredible! Usually called vanilla beans, we recommend that you blend a vanilla bean right into your chocolate drink or, even better, make a tea with a vanilla bean in it and use it as the base of your chocolate drink.

Only two of the fifty vanilla orchid species have commercial value, *Vanilla planifolia* and *Vanilla tahitensis*, but they all have the aphrodisiac magic. Vanilla's energy is female and so it combines naturally well with the male cacao. Vanilla orchids can actually naturally grow in cacao trees! In most mythologies, vanilla and cacao were divine lovers who eventually took plant form.

The Totonacs, who still survive in the Gulf coast region of their ancestors, in the modern Mexican state of Veracruz, gave both the vanilla bean, which they called *tlilxochitl*, and the orchid, *xanath*, major places in their religion and culture. According to Totonac myth, when the world was fresh and still frequented by deities, a beautiful young goddess, *Xanath*, visited the Earth and fell in love with a Totonac warrior. As a goddess — and daughter of the great goddess who ensured fertility — *Xanath* could not marry a mortal, but neither could she bring herself to abandon him. She ultimately resolved her predicament by bestowing herself upon her lover and his people in the form of the first vanilla vine. The blossoming and fruiting of this heavenly plant, so runs the myth, would provide the Totonacs a source of eternal happiness.

At least a thousand years ago the Totonacs worked out a means of processing the beans very much like the methods used today in commercial vanilla extraction, and they began to make vanilla an integral part of their culture. In addition to using it as a perfume and as a flavouring for food and drink, the Totonacs found that vanilla was effective as a medicine, an aphrodisiac and an insect repellent.

Other Old and New Friends of Cacao

Cacao has many old and new friends that have not quite made it to the inner circle yet. This list is by no means complete, and we thought we would list it anyway to provide hints and clues as to how to make the best chocolate drinks and treats ever, while having great fun!

Aloe Vera and Aloe Ferox

Aloe vera is a beautifying, longevity food of the highest order. The inner gel has great synergy with cacao when blended in drinks. The mucopolysaccharides in aloe vera contain monoatomic rhodium, a magical substance. Aloe makes cacao drinks creamier and gives more body and texture without detracting from the taste.

Aloe ferox is the Latin name for 'wild Aloe'. Aloe ferox belongs to the

Lilaceae plant family. It is neither irrigated nor treated with pesticides or insecticides. Containing three times as many polysaccharides than normal aloe vera, this plant is so strong that its survival is sustained through the strength of its own immune system. The proportion of amino acids (proteins) is two to one in comparison with aloe vera. It also contains considerably more iron and calcium.

Blue-Green Algae

Cacao is odd in that, as a nut, it has better synergy with algae (blue-green algae, spirulina, golden algae) than with green-leafy vegetables. Blue-green algae from Klamath Lake, Oregon has become a popular dried food among healthseekers the world over. This blue-green algae is a wild food with a fantastic array of brain-specific phytochemicals, a huge selection of antioxidants, minerals (especially zinc, selenium and magnesium), amino acids (it is a complete protein), vitamins, enzymes and many other unique nutrients.

A study looking at blue-green algae as brain food followed 109 students who were fed blue-green algae, and concluded that the children had a significant improvement in the ability to focus, follow directions and concentrate. In addition the children experienced a reduction in argumentative, demanding, and combative behaviour, fewer symptoms of anxiety and depression, an improvement in social skills, and fewer signs of emotional and behavioural withdrawal.

Blue-green algae is one of the richest food sources of antioxidant compounds, including carotenoids, chlorophyll and phycocyanin. These carotenoids include beta carotene, lycopene and lutein.

The antioxidant phycocyanin is a pigment that provides the intense blue colour in blue-green algae. It can constitute up to 15% of the dry weight of a blue-green algae harvest. Phycocyanin has intrinsic anti-inflammatory, liver protective and selective antitumor properties. Also found with the blue pigments in algae is a super-concentrated level of phenylethylamine (PEA).

Like cacao, blue-green algae seems to inhibit appetite and help people lose weight. In a double-blind crossover study involving human patients, supplementing the diets of obese individuals with 2.8 grams of blue-green algae three times daily over a four-week period resulted in a statistically significant reduction of body weight.

Cherries

Cherries are one of the best food sources of iron. Cherries are also a great source of antioxidants as well. The dark red pigments and flavourful sugars of fresh cherries make wonderful additions to your cacao cuisine. Yet the most incredible thing about cherries is their abnormally high concentration of the tryptamine, melatonin. As cacao naturally synergizes and activates tryptamines, we find deep spiritual and psychoactive significance in this combination. Try it yourself and see!

Citrus Fruits

Citrus has an interesting interaction with cacao. Sweet citrus juice does not mix well with cacao, however, the more bitter and sour juices of citrus do mix well. The solid matter of citrus also mixes well, such as lemon or lime peel. The essential oil of orange also has a beautiful synergy with cacao.

Durian

Durian captures the title as the most exotic of all fruits. Durian, like cacao, has psychoactive properties typically attributed to its high concentration of the tryptamine, tryptophan. The flesh of the fruit (each section looks like a pillow) is a fantastic taste mixture that reminds one of banana, cream and nuts, with a hint of onion.

Hemp Seed (Cannabis Seed)

Hemp and its seed have been used in medicine since about 2300 BCE, when the Chinese Emperor Shen-Nung prescribed *Chu-ma* (female hemp) for the treatment of beriberi, constipation, gout, malaria, menstrual problems and rheumatism. He classified *Chu-ma* as one of the Elixirs of Immortality. Besides its popularity in ancient China, the cultivation and use of hemp has been documented by many other great civilisations, including: Arabian, Egyptian, Indian, Medieval European, Persian, Roman and Sumerian. Hemp varieties were likely present and in common usage in the Americas when Columbus arrived.

Hemp seed is a complete protein. Hemp is not unique in having all the essential amino acids in its seed. Flax seeds also contain all the essential amino acids as do many other seeds. What is unique about hemp-seed protein is that 65% of it is globulin edestin — the highest found in the plant kingdom. The globulin edestin in hemp seed closely resembles that found in human blood plasma, and it is therefore easily digested, absorbed and utilised. Hemp edestin is so completely compatible with the human digestive system, that the Czechoslovakian Tubercular Nutrition Study (1955) found hemp seed to be the only food that can successfully treat the consumptive disease tuberculosis, in which the nutritive processes are impaired.

Additionally, phytosterols, of which hemp seed contains 438 mg/100g, have been shown to reduce total serum cholesterol by an average of 10% and low-density lipoprotein (LDL) cholesterol by an average of 13%. Hemp seed and the antioxidants in cacao work synergistically to reduce "bad" cholesterol.

In addition to containing the basic human nutrient groups, hemp foods have a high content of antioxidants (92.1 mg/100g) in the form of alpha-, beta-, gamma-, and delta-tocopherol and alpha-tocotrienol. These are all part of the vitamin E family. Cacao has tremendous synergy with the vitamin E family — especially creamy tocotrienols (rice bran) which add wonderful flavour and texture components to cacao cuisine, while increasing nutritional value.

Hempseed oil, in particular, is a favourite addition to the cacao beverage. Hempseed oil is one of the only food oils to contain the direct metabolites of the essential fatty acids (EFAs): linoleic and alpha-linolenic acids. The metabolites are gamma-linolenic acid (GLA) and stearidonic acid (SDA). Because of this, it can circumvent an impaired essential fatty acid metabolism and physical compromises arising from genetic factors, intake of too many other fats, aging and lifestyle patterns.

GLA (a unique omega 6 fatty acid found in spirulina and hemp seed) causes the body's inflammation response to be shut off.

Udo Erasmus, author of **Fats that Heal, Fats that Kill**, listed hemp seed as the number one food for human consumption found in nature in early editions of his book (of course, now we know that the number one food is actually cacao). At any rate, Udo Erasmus states that the proportions of linoleic acid (LA or omega 6) and linolenic acid (LNA or omega 3) in hemp seed oil are perfectly balanced to meet human requirements for essential fatty acids (EFAs), including gamma-linoleic acid (GLA). Unlike flaxseed oil and others, hempseed oil can be used continuously without developing a deficiency or other imbalance of EFAs. The peroxide value (PV, the degree of rancidity) of hempseed oil is only 0.1-0.5, which is very low and safe and does not spoil its taste. In comparison, the PV of virgin olive oil is about 20, and the PV of corn oil ranges from 40-60.

Mango

The mango refers to the fantastic fruit of India's favorite tree. More people on the earth have eaten mangos than apples. The mango has antiviral, antiseptic and antiparasitic properties. Mango, like papaya, adds the wonderful fruitiness of the tropics to all your cacao concoctions.

Noni

Noni is an exotic tropical fruit superfood, just like cacao! Fresh noni provides unlimited levels of energy, psychoactive effects, along with anti-inflammatory and medicinal properties. Noni gave the Polynesians the power and strength to explore the Pacific Ocean. Noni's magic is not just given away however; one must pay the admission fee of dealing with its intense spoiled-cheese odour and overpowering taste, but it's worth it!

Noni is one of our favourite additions to the chocolate beverage. Simply take the fresh and ripe or fermenting noni fruit and blend it with coconut water or simply water. Strain away the seeds and seed chunks. Then add cacao and

115

your other favourite ingredients. Fresh sugarcane juice works great as it masks the intense flavour and smell of the noni.

Papaya

Papaya is a great source of the protealytic enzyme *papain*. This enzyme is in greater concentrations in the unripe or half-ripe fruits as *papain* is the substance that protects the papaya from insect and bird predators. Papaya helps

to amplify cacao's zany, fruity character. The antiparasitical papaya seeds can be blended in with the papaya for a more peppery taste sensation.

Passion Fruit

Not only does passion fruit add nice fruity overtones to cacao concoctions, there also exists a synergistic relationship with cacao and the ground up seeds of passion fruit. The seeds of passion fruit contain a relaxing substance normally broken down by our digestive tract. However, it appears that some yet unnamed compound in cacao blocks the complete breakdown of this substance allowing its sedative effect to be felt. It is of note that members of the *Passiflora* genus contain monoamine oxidase inhibitors in the flowers and thus have entheogenic amplifying properties.

Pineapple

Pineapple is a great source of the anti-inflammatory enzyme *bromelain*. Pineapples are indigenous to the Americas. As far as an acid-fruit is concerned, pineapple has even better synergy with cacao than citrus fruits.

Raspberry

Raspberry has hormone influencing properties. The fruit is generally considered an aphrodisiac. The leaves or raspberry are often used medicinally as a tea to influence female hormone cycles. This tea and/or the fruit can be blended with cacao.

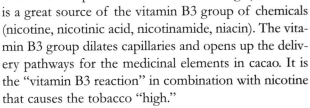

Tobacco

Tobacco (*Nicotiana spp.*) denotes a medicinal plant indigenous to the Americas which has become well-known for its abuses and excesses. Tobacco is perhaps the greatest shamanistic plant of them all. Tobacco is actually a powerful antiviral and antifungal medicine. Of course, chemical tobacco is a terrible artificial drug with cancer-causing properties. However, original tobacco (*Nicotiana rustica*) and organic tobacco varieties that are naturally dried may have completely different properties than chemical tobacco.

Tobacco tea was often used medicinally with cacao in past ages (careful, however, a tobacco tea made from ten cigarettes can kill a man. Usually one dry 3-4 centimeter leaf of tobacco per two liters of tea is enough!). Tobacco

is a great source of the vitamin B3 group of chemicals (nicotine, nicotinic acid, nicotinamide, niacin). The vitamin B3 group dilates capillaries and opens up the delivery pathways for the medicinal elements in cacao. It is the "vitamin B3 reaction" in combination with nicotine that causes the tobacco "high."

A book written in the 1500's by a Mayan priest (discovered in the Yucatan in 1914 and now at Princeton University) contains chants and incantations to be spoken over patients suffering from various diseases including skin eruptions, fever and seizures. A bowl of medicinal chocolate containing two peppers, honey and tobacco juice is prescribed.

What to do with Cacao Beans?

Step 1: Peel the cacao beans

Three methods of peeling:

1) Peel them dry with your fingernails or a small knife.

2) Soak the cacao beans in water for about 30 minutes, then peel them. Soaking softens the skin-peel and sometimes makes peeling easier.

3) Soak the cacao beans in water for 1 to 2 hours, then dehydrate them at low temperatures until the shells become crisp.

Step 2: Using your peeled cacao beans

1) Try eating them straight, one at a time. Chew it thoroughly and experience the taste extravaganza of raw chocolate.

2) Add to coconut-based or fruit-based smoothies to enhance the flavour.

3) Add a drip of agave cactus nectar or honey or other sweetening agent to the raw cacao bean and chew!

4) Freeze cacao beans with sweeteners (agave nectar or honey are fantastic). Eat cold.

5) Blend cacao beans into herbal teas with the Peruvian superfood maca.

6) Crush cacao beans with a mortar and pestle, then add to raw ice creams for the best chocolate chips in the world.

7) Create a raw chocolate bar! Blend the following raw ingredients together: cacao beans, agave cactus nectar, carob powder, maca, coconut oil and cashews. Pour into a mold and freeze. Eat cold and experience the truth about the food of the gods!

Warning: Eating cacao beans may cause you to have THE BEST DAY EVER!

Cacao is great fun for everyone — especially kids!

Refrigeration of cacao beans is not required.
Cacao beans keep well in cool, dry conditions.

The Cacaosphere: The mysterious realm where Heaven and Earth meet ... in the Heart (Heav-earth, Hea-rt).

The New Cacao Beverage

The general idea behind the new cacao beverage is blending peeled raw cacao in warm to hot water (usually some type of tea) or fresh coconut water and then adding some type of raw fat/oil and some type of raw sweetener and blending again.

Remember, if you are a beginner, keep it simple. If you are an advanced student of cacao alchemy, you can take it further.

When we are in the tropics we usually use fresh coconut water as the base for the drink. When we are in other climates we will usually use warm or hot herbal teas.

This drink is created in two parts. First create a tea. You can either make a water-infusion tea (soak the herbs in pure water in a glass container for 24 hours) or heat the tea lightly with the herbs in it and pure water (do not boil) for 20 minutes — keeping the tea at approximately 140 degrees Fahrenheit (60-65 degrees Celsius) is ideal.

Ingredients to Make 1.5 Litres of Tea

8 tablespoons of pau d'arco (South American herb, use dried powder or shavings)

3 tablespoons of cat's claw (South American herb, use dried powder or shavings)

1 raw vanilla bean (sliced and diced)

1 handful of goji berries (dried raisin-like superfruit)

Strain away the herbs and pour this warm tea into the base. The base should consist of the following ingredients in a blender:

20 cacao beans (preferably peeled) (Yes, this is raw chocolate...what we are really making here is chocolate milk without the cow!)

10 raw cashews (everyone loves cashews!)

3-5 tablespoons of maca (powdered root from Peru. An amazing hormonal superfood aphrodisiac, strengthener and fertility enhancer.)

3-5 tablespoons of agave cactus nectar or manuka honey

1-2 tablespoons of cold-pressed hempseed oil

1-2 tablespoons of coconut oil/butter

2-3 pinches of sea salt (such as Celtic sea salt or Himalayan pink rock salt)

2-4 pinches of powdered cinnamon and/or cayenne

Once the tea has been added to the base, then blend! You should have a foamy warm chocolate drink that will explode every taste sensation! Drink with your lover and experience an even heightened sense of pure pleasure!

If you do not know how to find any or all of the ingredients above, please visit: www.longevitywarehouse.com (in North America), www.detoxyourworld.com (in the United Kingdom) and/or your local healthfood store.

Additional tea ingredients could include:

Nettle leaf	Horsetail herb	Hemp leaf
Gingko leaf	Gotu Kola leaf	Salvia divinorum
Incan berries	Schizandra berries	Blue lotus

Other favourite foods to add to this drink include:

2 tablespoons of bee pollen

2 tablespoons of tocotrienols. Tocotrienols are an unheated, mechanically separated rice bran, full of potent antioxidants.

2-3 tablespoons of spirulina. One of the most nutritious foods on Earth and a sacred food of the Aztecs.

1-2 tablespoons of purple corn extract. Over 90% pure antioxidants.

3-4 tablespoons of mesquite powder. This is the powder of the desert mesquite pod. It enhances creaminess and adds minerals and blood sugar balancing elements.

5-8 peppercorns. Pepper is not just for salad anymore.

Supplements to add to cacao drinks include:

If you consume a large amount of chocolate and/or cacao, we recommend that you consider including the following supplements in your chocolate alchemy, with your chocolate drink or in your diet:

• Calcium (1/2 ounce of liquid angstrom calcium per liter of chocolate beverage or per 30 cacao beans) — Liquid angstrom calcium is a fantastic addition to your cacao alchemy. Angstrom calcium is the best source of supplemental calcium, even better than coral calcium. Calcium has a unique effect on cacao, perhaps it is the synergy of calcium with the magnesium in the cacao. Calcium helps to sweeten and smooth the taste of cacao. Central Americans often grind the seeds of a relative of *Theobroma cacao* called *Theobroma bicolor* with lime (a naturally-occuring calcium-rich powdery rock) to make a creamy, tasty treat.

- 1,500-2,000 mg of the amino acid Lysine. Lysine balances the high arginine content of chocolate and/or cacao. This amino acid decreases cacao's sexually stimulating elements. It also decreases the chance of viral outbreaks. Arginine is aggravating to those with herpes problems; however, raw cacao is much gentler (less aggravating to herpes) than cooked cacao and processed chocolate. Lysine replaces arginine in the viral replication process and inhibits the duplication of the virus. For those with herpes, we recommend looking into raw-food nutrition (**Detox Your World** by Shazzie and **The Sunfood Diet Success System** by Wolfe would be great places to learn about raw food) and oxygen therapies (**Flood Your Body With Oxygen** by Ed McCabe is a great book to start with).

- 1-2 teaspoon(s) of methyl-sulphonyl-methane (MSM) powder crystals. MSM is simply one of the greatest discoveries in nutritional history. MSM increases the absorption of minerals, vitamins and amino acids. The youthening powers of MSM are exceptional.

- 300-600 mg of MegaHydrate™. This is a product developed by our friend Dr. Patrick Flanagan. It protects all the nutrients in your drink from oxidation. Essentially, it helps preserve the drink longer and helps deliver the nutrients to your cells without metabolic loss.

- 100-300 mg of Vitamin B3 (Niacin) — Niacin can increase the absorption of the cacao drink. It also amplifies the brain-enhancing effect of cacao.

- 1-2 mg of Vitamin B6 — Helps to enhance the brainpower effects of cacao. Alternatively to supplement B6, spirulina and goji berries are great natural sources of this vitamin.

- 50-200 mg of Co-enzyme Q-10 — A great supplement for heart strength. Many people with heart troubles will naturally gravitate to cacao and Co-Q10 due to the overwhelming evidence connecting cacao to heart health.

All alone I sing
To the one who is my Lord:
In this place where the gods command,
The flower-chocolate drink is foaming — the flower intoxication.

I yearn, oh yes!
For my heart has tasted it:
It intoxicated my heart — songs, dreams, yearnings.
My heart has tasted it.

— **Tlaltecatzin, Aztec poet**

the recipes...

Commonly Used Kitchen Equipment

Again, we may use some items that you don't have, so here is a list of what they are and how you can substitute them with the items you do have. Some of the machines are very heavy duty, and can be substituted with a less powerful machine that you just have to use for a short while longer. Heavy-duty expensive equipment is lovely to use, but it's not totally necessary. In the recipes, we always offer alternatives to the expensive equipment route.

Here is a list of equipment commonly used in these recipes. If you can't find these items in the shops, have a look at the resources at the back of the book.

Juicers

Juicers can range from the $75 (£40 in the UK) centrifugal variety, to the $400+ (£200+ in the UK) masticating variety. We always advise people to start off with the centrifugal one, and when they want to move on, they have a gift to give that will help to start someone else on this food revolution. There are also citrus juicers, and we'd advise that you get yourself one of these if you juice a lot of citrus. It means you don't have to peel the fruit first which saves you a lot of time.

Mandoline

Another manual gadget; the mandolin slices, chips and juliennes. It's great if you have a family, as it can whizz through vegetables at a very fast rate. Some food processors work in a similar way with their various attachments, so check what you already have first.

Blender

Normal blenders and bullet blenders (Magic Bullet, Nutri-Bullet) are capable of doing most things you want it to, such as blending soups, smoothies and dips. However, the high-powered Vita-Mix really comes into its own when you want to blend large amounts of thicker, harder items. It can pulverise carrots and make a "juice" out of the whole vegetable. It's a blender which is hard to beat. Because it's a commercial blender rather than a domestic one, don't be surprised at the $400+ (£500+ in the UK) price tag. When we suggest using a spice mill to grind foods, you can use your Vita-Mix dry jug if you have one. Likewise, when we suggest using a hand blender, a Vita-Mix wet jug will work quicker. We don't suggest these automatically as we're not assuming you have the Vita-Mix. However, if you want one, then Shazzie's company in the UK and David's company in the USA both stock and recommend them.

Hand blender

Also known as a liquidiser, this is the type that you hold and push into the food, whizzing it up in the process. It's great if you don't have a Nutri-Bullet or Vita-Mix, as it will blend thicker food than your blender will manage. You can buy them for about $10 (£5 in the UK), but that type seems to have a tiny blade which doesn't do the job very well. Go for the ones which are about $35 (£20 in the UK) and have larger blades that point both up and down.

Food processor

This machine revolutionises the preparation of raw food. Make pies, crackers and pâtés in minutes. With the many types on the market, look for one with a large basin and a fast speed, as it will make a difference to the convenience of your food preparation.

Spice/Coffee mill

If you have a food processor with a blender or a solo blender, you might already have one of these. If not, you can buy them quite cheaply. They are fantastic for making small amounts of really smooth dressings and for milling dry seeds.

Dehydrator

A few of the recipes here call for a dehydrator. This is a machine like a cool oven that blows warm, but not hot, air over the food. The food changes in structure as water is removed, but enzymes and other heat sensitive nutrients aren't lost in the process. We dehydrate at around 105-115 degrees Fahrenheit (40-46 degrees Celsius), and use Teflex sheets (a thick type of wax paper) for the more liquidy recipes. If you don't have a dehydrator, you can achieve similar results by putting your oven on its lowest setting and leaving the door open, or using an airing cupboard or the sunshine.

Icons

We've added icons to each recipe, so you can see at a glance the equipment you'll need.

Trans-Atlantic Translations

Because Americans wear their pants on the outside, they also use some other words differently. Here are the common food words which differ between us.

coriander = cilantro
dessertspoon = 2 teaspoons
courgette = zucchini
beansprouts = sprouts
spring onions = green onions
chips = fries
chick peas = garbanzos
cling film = Saran wrap
stoned = pitted
punnet = plastic fruit basket, about 2-3 cups
little gem = tiny lettuce, like a mini-romaine

aubergine = eggplant
sharon fruit = persimmon
rocket = arugula
sweetcorn = corn/maize
crisps = chips
beetroot = beet
pepper = bell pepper
physalis = cape gooseberry

Water

Where we mention water, you can either use your preferred water (we use mineral water), the freshly-squeezed juice of a cucumber or celery, or the water from a young or old coconut, depending on whether the dish is sweet or savoury. We never drink or soak dried products in water straight from the tap.

Chocolate Powder and Cacao

Where we mention chocolate powder as a recipe ingredient, we are referring to raw, organic chocolate beans or cacao nibs that you have ground yourself using a coffee/spice mill or pestle and mortar. If you don't have these beans/nibs, then using a good-quality, organic cocoa powder will also work, but will feel different in your body. We wholeheartedly recommend that you use finely-crushed raw, organic cacao beans/nibs in these recipes.

Powdered Green Superfood

We use this in a couple of recipes. Nature's Living Superfood, Pure Synergy and Nature's First Food are all great brands to use. Spirulina or Klamath Lake Blue-green Algae works great here too.

Almond Chewy Squares

Makes about 16 yummy chewys.

1 cup of almonds, soaked 2-4 hours

12 dried apricots, soaked 1 hour

1 dessertspoon of poppy seeds

1 teaspoon of mixed spices (allspice, nutmeg, etc.)

2 dessertspoons of chocolate powder (crushed cacao beans or nibs)

1 heaped teaspoon of spirulina

1 dessertspoon of soak water from the apricots

Add all ingredients to a food processor and blend until the mixture has formed a stiff ball. If it doesn't stick together, add some of the apricot soak water. Lay the mixture out onto a Teflex sheet, and press it out to 6-8mm thick. Square off the edges.

Dehydrate for four hours, when it should be ready to turn over and remove the Teflex sheet. Do this, then score the square shapes, about 2x2 inches.

Dehydrate for a further four hours, then enjoy!

Cinnamon Rolls

Makes 10 of these gorgeous moreish little bites.

1 serving of **Dark Chocolate Sauce** (see page 140)
Cinnamon, ground
1 cup of pecans, not soaked
1 cup of medjool dates, stoned

Blend the pecans and dates together in a food processor to make a dough. Dust some cinnamon onto a clean work surface, and place the dough on it. Sprinkle some more cinnamon on top of the dough and flatten it out, adding more cinnamon if it ever gets sticky.

Once the dough is about 4 mm thick, and about 15 x 15 cm square, cut the edges so they are neat. Spread the chocolate sauce evenly on top.

Pick up one side of the dough and start to roll to the other side, so you end up with a spiralled log. Cut this log into 1.5 cm wide rolls and serve.

Green Coconut and Durian Soup

Serves 2

2 young Thai coconuts (water and jelly)

1 tablespoon of powdered green superfood

1 level teaspoon of coconut oil

2 real vitamin C capsules (powdered camu camu or acerola berries)

1 heaped tablespoon of chocolate powder (crushed cacao beans or nibs)

1/2 cup of fresh durian

5 almonds, skinned

1 tablespoon of maca

Drain the coconuts through the tops, then cut the tops off so you can use them to serve the soup in. We make ours into lotus flowers, simply by cutting from the top down with a sharp knife all the way around. We then put a pointed knife about 4 cm down from the tip onto the coconut. Holding the coconut and knife steady with one hand, we bang the top of the knife repeatedly with the other. Once we crack the coconut, we pry open the lid by carefully sliding the knife around as it cracks.

Add 1.5 coconuts' worth of water and jelly into a blending jug. You can save some of the unused jelly for decoration if you like. Remove the vitamin C powder from the capsules, and add that to the jug. Add all the other ingredients except the almonds, and blend until it's all smooth.

Make sure there is no jelly in either of the coconuts, and then pour equal amounts of the soup into the coconuts. Split the almonds in half and place them in a flower pattern in each bowl. Add a tiny pinch of ground cacao on top, then serve.

The Great Glass Elevator

If you've read Shazzie's book Detox Your World, *you may have already experienced The Best Meal in the World. Here it is with a chocolatey twist. And twist you it will! Serves 2.*

1 young coconut

30 cacao beans, skinned

1 durian

2 people

A ball pond (a pool of plastic balls you find at amusement parks!)

Cut the top off the coconut and add two straws. Open the durian. Eat the durian and cacao until they're all gone, without fighting over the durian. Sip from the coconut, together. This will give you a major chakra rush and make you go all funny! After finishing the coconut water, enjoy your post multiple duriasmic chill by lolling about in your ball pond for an hour before resuming any adult respon-sibilities that you may have. Believe me, you won't be able to do anything else.

Powerful Sticky Nuts

Serves 8 snack portions.

5 cups of walnuts, soaked 4-8 hours

1 cup of cashew nuts

1 cup of goji berries, soaked 1-4 hours

1 cup of raw agave nectar

4 tablespoons of chocolate powder (crushed cacao beans or nibs)

1 tablespoon of powdered nettles or powdered green superfood

1 teaspoon of spirulina powder

Break the cashews with a food processor, to create small pieces, a bit bigger than crumbs.

Blend the agave nectar, goji berries and powders together. Add the cashews and walnuts and stir until the walnuts are fully coated. Pour onto a Teflex sheet (Teflon-coated wax-like paper), spread out until the walnuts are separated, and dehydrate for 4-8 hours. The result will be sticky, yet crunchy walnuts with a kick to keep you going through the day.

Papaya Cheezes

Serves 4 snack portions.

1 medium papaya

1/2 cup of raw agave nectar

1 cup of cashew nuts

4 tablespoons chocolate powder

1 tablespoon of hemp seeds, shelled (hemp nuts)

1 teaspoon of fresh lime zest, finely grated

Cut the papaya in half and scoop out the seeds in the middle. Using a vegetable peeler, peel the skin from the papaya and discard. Thinly slice the papaya and place the slices individually on a Teflex sheet.

Blend the cashews, chocolate, lime and agave nectar until super-smooth. Pour this onto the papaya slices, allowing it to dribble all over. Sprinkle the hemp seeds on top. Dehydrate for about 8 hours. You'll get a very unusual and beautiful sweet cheese-like finger snack — it goes great with grapes.

Blackies

This is like a brownie, only darker and much richer. You can't eat many of these in one go, unless you're a greedy guts.

4 cups of black mission figs, soaked 1 hour

1 cup of black tahini

1/2 cup of chocolate powder (crushed cacao beans or nibs)

1 cup of goji berries, soaked 1 hour

1 dessertspoon of fresh mint leaves

1 tablespoon of golden flax seeds

Pinch of Celtic sea salt

Finely grind the flax seeds in a coffee mill, Nutri-Bullet or Vita-Mix dry jug. Put all the ingredients into a food processor and process until fine and dough-like. If the mixture doesn't stick together, add slowly some goji berry soak water whilst blending.

Knead the dough until you've put lots of love into it, and then place it onto a Teflex sheet. Spread it out until it's about 2 cm thick, and square the edges off. Cut into little squares. If you fancy it, place half a cherry on top of each square.

Dehydrate for about 4 hours, then turn onto the dehydrator tray without a Teflex sheet, and dehydrate for 6 more hours.

Raspberry Berets

A tribute to Prince, the man with the chocolate voice. Serves 2.

24 raspberries

1 portion of **Dark Chocolate Sauce**

So simple... Pour little amounts of the sauce into the cavities at the top of the raspberries. Put in the freezer for an hour or so, and they'll become sweet crunchy surprises.

Oh, I forgot to mention, you have to sing all the time you're making this: "She wore a Raspberry beret, The kind u find in a second hand store, Raspberry beret, And if it was warm she wouldn't wear much more, Raspberry beret, I think I love her..." And we think we love Prince.

Prince Pondicherry's Cherry Cake

This cake is so amazing and yummy, it's fit for royalty — And you!

Base

1 level teaspoon dried orange zest

3 cups of baby figs (dried)

1 cup of almonds (soaked in water for 1 hour)

1 cup of almonds (dry)

1/4 teaspoon of ginger powder

1/4 teaspoon of grated nutmeg

1 cup of dried cherries

2 cups of fresh cherries

1/2 cup of poppy seeds

Jam

2 cups of fresh cherries, stoned

1 level dessertspoon of chocolate powder (crushed cacao beans or nibs)

6 prunes (dry), stoned

Cream

3 cups of cashews (dry)

Juice of 1-2 oranges

1 tablespoon of water

1 vanilla pod

To make the base

Blend all the base ingredients together in a food processor until a ball forms. You might have to do this in two batches as it's quite large.

Line a lose-bottomed cake tin with cling film (Saran wrap) and put half the mixture into the tin, then flatten it out. Turn this out onto a serving plate. Put the remaining mixture in the tin, and flatten it out. Leave it in the tin until you've completed the next step.

To make the jam

Blend all the jam ingredients with a hand blender or in a Nutri-Bullet or Vita-Mix. Add more prunes if it's not solid enough.

To make the cream

Cut the vanilla pod into tiny pieces. Blend all the cream ingredients together using a hand blender. You could start the mixture off in a food processor, and then use a blender once the cashews have broken down. Alternatively, if you have a Nutri-Bullet or Vita-Mix, you can easily make the cream all in one go.

To complete the cake

Spread half the jam onto the cake base. Spread half the cream onto the cake base. Turn out the other half of the cake and place it on top of the spread cream. Spread the rest of the jam on the top of the cake. Spread the rest of the cream on top of the jam. Decorate with cherries and a deep red rose.

Violet's Violent End

Serves 8 generous portions.

Pastry

1 cup of oat groats

1 cup of almonds (dry)

1 cup of dried apricots, soaked in water for 2-4 hours

Filling

2 cups of cashew nuts, dry

2 cups of fresh blueberries

2 tablespoons of raw agave nectar

2 tablespoons of chocolate powder (crushed cacao beans or nibs)

To make the pastry

Grind the almonds and oat groats into a fine flour, using a Nutri-Bullet, Vita-Mix dry jug or a coffee mill. Transfer to a food processor, saving about 1 tablespoon for rolling the pastry out. Switch the food processor on, and drop the apricots down the chute (this is what happened to that naughty Verucca Salt, too!). As the apricots are blended, a dough-like consistency should form. If it doesn't, add some soak water from the apricots. Once the mixture has formed into a ball, switch the machine off and remove the dough.

Place some of your saved flour onto a chopping board. Put the dough on this, and then add some more flour onto the dough. Start to flatten and roll the pastry, as you would any other pastry. Make it wide enough to add to an eight inch tart dish. Once rolled, line your tart dish with cling-film, and place the pastry on top of that. Press the pastry into the dish, and cut the edges off. Flute the edges.

Place the tart dish in a dehydrator for 2 hours. The pastry will harden slightly. Carefully remove the pastry from the dish, by turning it upside down. Remove the cling film (Saran wrap). Put the formed shell back on a dehydrator tray and dehydrate for 2 more hours. Removing it from the dish like this enables more warm air to reach the underside of the pastry, and crisps it up.

When your pastry shell is ready, remove it from the dehydrator and put it to one side.

To make the filling

Add the remaining ingredients, except one cup of blueberries to a Vita-Mix or high-powered blender. Blend all the ingredients until the cashews are completely broken down and the mixture is smooth.

Pour this mixture into your pastry and spread it to the edges. Place the remaining blueberries on top, in a beautiful pattern. Put this into a freezer for at least an hour before serving.

This keeps for many weeks in a freezer, just defrost it for half an hour before cutting and serving.

Dark Chocolate Sauce

We use this to top every sweet dish going. We also add it to smoothies, and just dip our fingers in it and eat as is. Yum yum.

4 heaped tablespoons of chocolate powder (crushed cacao beans or nibs)

3 tablespoons of raw agave nectar

1/2 teaspoon of coconut oil

Mix all the ingredients together to form a paste. If you need it runnier, add more agave nectar. If you need it creamier, add some more coconut oil. We love to make this in a pestle and mortar, as we feel more love going into it.

Light Chocolate Sauce

A much milder version than that above, but still with a wonderful chocolate taste.

1 teaspoon of chocolate powder (crushed cacao beans or nibs)

1 dessertspoon of coconut oil

1 cup of macadamia nuts

1 cup of young coconut water

The jelly of 1 young coconut

Seeds from half a vanilla pod

Blend all ingredients using a Nutri-Bullet or other high-powered blender until the nuts are broken down and the sauce is smooth.

Chocolate Caramel Sauce

1 cup of macadamia nuts

1 tablespoon of chocolate powder (crushed cacao beans or nibs)

1 cup of **Almond Mylk** (see page 196)

2 tablespoons of raw agave nectar

5 medjool dates, stoned

Blend everything until smooth and creammmmmmy. To make it extra smooth, strain the sauce through a sieve.

Chocolate Mylk Kick

Serves 2, though you may find yourself making more!

1 pint of very cold **Almond Mylk** (see page 196)

4 tablespoons of chocolate powder (crushed cacao beans or nibs)

2 tablespoons of carob powder

1 teaspoon of maca powder

1 teaspoon of tocotrienols

4 tablespoons of raw agave nectar

1/4 teaspoon of powdered ginseng

1 teaspoon of cold-pressed hemp oil

1 teaspoon of cold-pressed flax oil

Blend all the ingredients together and enjoy immediately before we come over and drink it for you!

Cacao, Hemp and Banana Shake

This is a great not-too-sweet drink, containing lots of life-giving stuff. Serves 2.

1 ripe banana, peeled

1 young coconut

1 dessertspoon of chocolate powder (crushed cacao beans or nibs)

2 dessertspoons of cold-pressed hemp seeds

1 teaspoon of cold-pressed hemp oil

Open the coconut in your preferred way. Pour the liquid and scoop the jelly into your blender. Add all the other ingredients and blend until smooth.

Rich Calcium Shake

I'm not a big fan of sesame, but this drink does it for me big time. Little 'uns also love this. If it's too bitter, add some raw agave nectar or some dates and blend again. We didn't photograph the following two drinks as they didn't look much different to the other drinks in this book! Please forgive us, for we know not what we do. Serves 2.

1 cup of sprouted sesame seeds

1 young coconut

4 tablespoons of angstrom/ionic calcium

1 tablespoon of chocolate powder (crushed cacao beans or nibs)

2 cups of water

6 apricot kernels (for that real almondy taste)

Open the coconut in your preferred way. Pour the liquid and scoop the jelly into your blender. Add all the other ingredients and blend until smooth.

You may want to strain this after blending for a smoother shake — this will depend upon the strength of your blender as well as your preferences.

Chocovanilla Shake

Simple, yet totally gorgeous and energising. Serves 2-3.

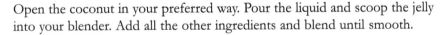

2 young coconuts

1 vanilla bean

1 tablespoon of chocolate powder (crushed cacao beans or nibs)

Open the coconut in your preferred way. Pour the liquid and scoop the jelly into your blender. Add all the other ingredients and blend until smooth.

If you don't have a strong blender such as the Vita-Mix, you may prefer to split the vanilla bean down the middle, scrape the seeds into the blender and discard the tougher skin. This is why we recommend the Vita-Mix, it could pulverise your socks! Er, don't try that, please.

Mr Slugworth

This is the most mineral-rich shot in the world! Get it down your neck quick and enjoy the rush! Serves 1.

1 teaspoon of Klamath Lake Crystals (dried blue-green algae)

1 teaspoon of cold-pressed hemp oil

1/2 teaspoon of chocolate powder (crushed cacao beans or nibs)

1 dessertspoon of raw agave nectar

1 teaspoon of lemon juice

1 dessertspoon of ionic/angstrom Water of Life or Mineral of Life

Mix everything together and serve in a shot glass with a slice of lemon. Wow!

Grandpa Joe on the Go

If you need a little helping hand, then make this, sit back and relax. For a bit... Serves 1.

A squeeze of lemon juice

1 cup of water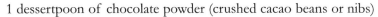

20 soaked almonds

1 dessertpoon of chocolate powder (crushed cacao beans or nibs)

4 prunes, soaked 2-4 hours and stoned

1 dessertspoon of prune soak water

1 dessertspoon of raw agave nectar

Add all the ingredients to a blender and blend. Strain (the drink!) into a serving glass.

Hot Chocolate

Entice your loved ones with this warm, creamy and smooth delight. Makes 4 cups.

1 pint of **Almond Mylk** (see page 196), made with warm water
4 tablespoons of chocolate powder (crushed cacao beans or nibs)
2 tablespoons of raw agave nectar

Blend all ingredients in a blender and serve immediately. For a hotter chocolate, make the almond mylk with half the amount of water. Blend all the ingredients, then add half a pint of hot water, whisk and serve.

Chocolate del Diablo

Kicks you like a mule. Makes 4 cups.

1 pint of **Almond Mylk** (see page 196), made with warm water
4 tablespoons of chocolate powder (crushed cacao beans or nibs)
2 tablespoons of raw agave nectar
1/4 teaspoon cayenne pepper
Pinch each of mace, nutmeg and cinnamon

Blend all ingredients in a blender and serve immediately. For a hotter chocolate, make the almond mylk with half the amount of water. Blend all the ingredients, then add half a pint of hot water, whisk and serve.

Chocolate Bar

You will love this! These bars have a lower melting point than traditional chocolate, so we keep ours in the freezer. We use ice-cube trays, as they make nice portions, but do improvise with lots of different shapes and moulds. You can even make chocolate bunnies for Easter!

1 level tablespoon of coconut oil

2 heaped tablespoons of chocolate powder (crushed cacao beans or nibs)

1 level tablespoon of raw agave nectar

1 heaped tablespoon of tocotrienols

1 level dessertspoon of maca powder

Blend everything until very smooth. Pour into your chosen mould, freeze for about 20-30 minutes, then live and go to heaven!

Chocolate Bar II

1 cup of chocolate powder (crushed cacao beans or nibs)

1 cup of raw agave nectar

1 cup of carob powder

1/2 cup of coconut oil

1 dessertspoon of ionic/angstrom calcium

1 cup of cashew nuts

Blend everything until very smooth. Pour into your chosen mould, freeze for about 20-30 minutes, then live and go to heaven!

Life by Chocolate

Shazzie and our good friend Daniel invented this major chocolate experience. It's got everything a chocoholic could wish for, and when you put as much love in it as we did, it gets that extra special sparkle!

Base

1/4 cup of carob powder

2 cups of pecans (dry)

20 black mission figs, soaked in water 4-8 hours (keep the water)

Pinch of sea salt

1/2 teaspoon of cinnamon

1/4 teaspoon of nutmeg

1/4 teaspoon of allspice

Middle

1.5 cups of avocado

1.5 cups of coconut jelly

1/4 cup of tocotreinols

1 dessertspoon of maca

1/2 cup of carob powder

1/2 cup of chocolate powder (crushed cacao beans or nibs)

1/2 cup of raw agave nectar

Pinch of cayenne pepper

Topping

1 dessertspoon of orange zest

1/2 cup of chocolate powder (crushed cacao beans or nibs)

1/2 cup of raw agave nectar

1/4 cup of soak water from the black mission figs

To make the base

In a Vita-Mix dry jug or coffee mill, grind the nuts to a powder with the spices, salt and carob powder. Add this to the food processor with most of the figs and process the ingredients until they have broken down. Add the rest of the figs one by one as you're processing to get a hard dough-like consistency. Put this into an eight inch pie dish, and flatten evenly. Place this in the freezer.

To make the middle

Blend all the middle ingredients until smooth and pour this onto the base. Return the two-staged pie to the freezer.

To make the topping

Mix all the topping ingredients except the orange zest with a spoon until smooth. Spoon this on the pie in drips or spread it all over. Decorate with the zest and some extra whole chocolate beans.

Chocolate Fudge

Makes about 30-40 pieces

2 cups of cashews nuts, soaked
1 cup of dates, stoned and soaked
1 cup of raisins, soaked
1 cup of chocolate powder (crushed cacao beans or nibs)
1/2 cup of water
1/2 cup of golden flax seeds, ground
1/2 cup of carob powder

Add all ingredients into the food processor, except the ground flax seeds. Process until very smooth. Add the ground flax seeds and process again until you can't see the flax.

Scrape the mixture into a three quarter inch deep tin (with greaseproof paper if you wish), and spread it evenly. Freeze for two hours. Cut into 1 inch squares and freeze for a further hour before removing and eating.

Try serving this with **Dark Chocolate Sauce** as a dip.

Fudge Reloaded

Makes about 30-40 pieces

1 cup of dates, stoned and soaked for 1-2 hours

1.5 cups date soak water

1 vanilla pod

2.5 cups of almonds

2 tablespoons of chocolate powder (crushed cacao beans or nibs)

1/2 cup of dried shredded coconut

Add all ingredients into the food processor. Process until very smooth.

Scrape the mixture into a three-quarter inch deep tin (with greaseproof paper if you wish), and spread it evenly. Freeze for two hours. Cut into 1 inch squares and freeze for a further hour before removing and eating.

Try serving this with **Dark Chocolate Sauce** as a dip.

Cosmic Pepperman's Raw Chocolate Chip Pistachio Mint Ice Cream

Big thanks to Jackie Ayala and Dave Steinberg (Cosmic Pepper Productions) for offering this stunning dessert to the world. Serves 4-8.

Pulp from 5 young Thai coconuts

Water from 3 young coconuts

1 cup raw pistachios

1/2 cup of shelled raw hemp seeds (hemp nuts)

1 cup macadamia nuts

1/2 cup of raw agave nectar

1 tablespoon of Hawaiian white honey

1 tablespoon of spirulina

1 medium ripe avocado

3 tablespoons of chopped fresh mint (chocolate mint is preferable)

2 tablespoons of coconut oil/butter

2-4 tablespoons of raw cacao nibs

2 drops of peppermint essential oil

1 tablespoon of dried powdered nettles (optional)

Blend the coconut pulp and water in a Nutri-Bullet, Vita-Mix or other high-powered blender. Strain through a fine mesh strainer or nut milk bag.

Pour the coconut blend back into the blender and add the rest of the ingredients except the cacao and peppermint oil.

Blend on high until creamy.

Stir in the cacao and oil by hand.

For best results chill in the freezer for several hours, then pour into an ice cream maker and follow the ice cream maker's directions. If you don't have an ice cream maker, stir the mixture every hour and return to the freezer until solid.

Speckled Ice Cream Mould with Blackcurrant Coulis

Serves 2.

3 bananas, chopped small and frozen overnight
1 teaspoon of coconut oil/butter
1/2 cup of chocolate nibs, ground but not powdered
1/4 cup of blackcurrants
2 tablespoons of raw agave nectar

Blend the agave nectar and blackcurrants together and leave this coulis to marinate while preparing the rest of the dish.

Add the frozen bananas and coconut oil to the food processor and process until the mixture becomes white. You may have to stop and rest your machine as it takes a few minutes. Scrape down the banana halfway, and work quickly so the bananas don't melt, otherwise they won't turn to white whippy-like ice cream.

Once the ice cream is made, mix in the chocolate by hand and put the ice cream into two small ramekin dishes. Return these to the freezer for about an hour.

Strain the blackcurrant skin and pips out of the coulis using some muslin. Discard the skin and pips. Once the ice cream is ready to be served, drizzle the coulis on your serving plates. Very briefly dunk the ramekins in hot water, and turn the ice creams out onto the plates. Use a knife around the outsides if you need to. It might be best if you turn it out onto a plain plate, and then carefully transfer it to your plate that has the coulis on.

Chocolate Chip Oat Cookies

Makes 12.

1 cup of oat groats (soaked for 2 days; change water 4 times in this period)

1 cup of dry oat groats, finely ground to a powder

1 cup of dried apricots, soaked overnight

1 cup of broken raw cacao bean pieces or cacao nibs

Put both types of oats and the apricots in the food processor and process until everything is well mixed together and the apricots have broken down. Stir in the cacao pieces by hand. Divide the mixture into 12, and dollop on to Teflex sheets. Shape the mixture to look like cookies and dehydrate for 8-10 hours. They don't have to be hard all the way through, so keep testing them!

Black Forest Cookies

Makes 24.

1 cup of oat groats (soaked for 2 days; change water 4 times in this period)

1 cup of dry oat groats, finely ground to a powder

1 cup of dried apricots, soaked overnight

1 cup of cashew nuts, soaked 2-4 hours

1 cup of broken raw cacao bean pieces or cacao nibs

2 cups of mixed fruit such as black cherries, blueberries, blackberries, blackcurrants and black grapes.

Put both types of oats along with the cashews and fruit in the food processor and process until everything is well mixed together and the apricots have broken down. Stir in the cacao pieces by hand. Divide the mixture into 12, and dollop on to Teflex sheets. Shape the mixture to look like cookies and dehydrate for 8-10 hours. They don't have to be hard all the way through, so keep testing them!

Mint and Chocolate Chip Ice Cream

Serves 4.

4 bananas, chopped small and frozen overnight

1 teaspoon of coconut butter/oil

1 cup of broken raw cacao bean pieces or cacao nibs

4 tablespoons of raw agave nectar

1 cup of fresh mint leaves

The day before you make this, finely chop the mint and add to the agave nectar. Leave it to marinate overnight. Using a fine cloth, strain the liquid from the pulp. You can use the discarded mint pulp in a dressing or sauce. You can keep the liquid for several days in the fridge.

Add the frozen bananas and coconut oil to the food processor and process until the mixture becomes white. You may have to stop and rest your machine as it takes a few minutes. Scrape down the banana halfway, and work quickly so the bananas don't melt, otherwise they won't turn to white whippy-like ice cream.

Once the ice cream is made, mix in the chocolate chips and the minty agave nectar by hand. Serve scoops of this immediately or return it to the freezer where it will keep for about a week.

Happy Lemon Boats

Sail away in your Happy Lemon Boat down the chocolate river of your dreams. Serves 4.

1/2 cup of chocolate powder (crushed cacao beans or nibs)

3 lemons

1 avocado, stoned and peeled

1/2 cup of carob powder

10 dates, stoned and soaked

4 tablespoons of raw agave nectar

Cut two of the lemons in half, lengthways. Scoop the flesh out, being careful to keep the skins intact. Cut a tiny strip off the bottom of each lemon half, so that they will sit flat on a plate without falling over. Finely chop these cut-off strips and add them to a blender jug. Juice a quarter of the scooped out lemon flesh and add that juice to the blender jug.

Discard the rest of the lemon flesh. Blend the ingredients in the jug with the chocolate powder, avocado, carob powder, dates and agave nectar until smooth and creamy. If it tastes too bitter, add more agave nectar.

Divide the mixture into four, and pile it into the boats.

Cut up the third lemon to create sails, and add one to each boat.

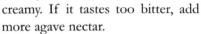
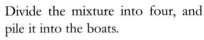
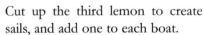
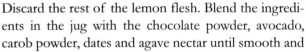

Cacao Kapow

Don't be fooled by the simplicity of this meal, it's one of our best ever recipes! Serves 2, and keeps you up all day.

2 oranges

14 dried apricots, soaked in water 4-6 hours

1/2 cup almonds, dry

1 dessertspoon of chocolate powder (crushed cacao beans or nibs)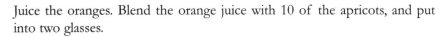

2 dessertspoons of **Dark Chocolate Sauce** (see page 140)

Juice the oranges. Blend the orange juice with 10 of the apricots, and put into two glasses.

Blend the remaining apricots with the almonds, chocolate sauce and chocolate powder. Keep it still slightly crunchy. Spoon this on top of the orange and apricot blend.

For an extra treat, top with some agave nectar and some orange zest. Wow!

Mini Spicy Cookies

Makes about 12.

4 bananas

1/4 cup of golden flax seed

1/2 cup of chocolate powder (crushed cacao beans or nibs)

2 cups of sunflower seeds

1 cup of sesame seeds

1/2 cup of oat groats

4 dates, stoned and soaked

1 tablespoon of raw agave nectar

1 heaped teaspoon of mixed spices (allspice, nutmeg, etc.)

1 heaped teaspoon of cinnamon

1 heaped teaspoon of Chinese five spice

Mill the sesame seeds, oat groats and flax seeds until they become a fine "flour". Put three of the bananas into a food processor with the sunflower seeds and agave nectar, and process until the mixture is blended. Add this mixture to a mixing bowl.

Dice the dates and remaining banana and add those to the mixture. Gradually mix in the flour and spices until everything is evenly mixed.

Press the mixture out onto a chopping board until it's about 1 cm thick. Using a small cookie cutter, cut as many cookies as you can. Roll the remaining mixture back up, press it out and cut again. Continue until there's no mixture left. Dehydrate until crisp, about 8 hours, turning over once halfway through.

Chocolate Banana Bread

Makes 2 loaves.

4 bananas

1/4 cup of golden flax seed

1/2 cup of chocolate powder (crushed cacao beans or nibs)

2 cups of sunflower seeds

1 cup of sesame seeds

1/2 cup of oat groats

4 dates, soaked and stoned

1 tablespoon of raw agave nectar

Mill the sesame seeds, oat groats and flax seeds until they become a fine "flour". Put three of the bananas into a food processor with the sunflower seeds and agave nectar, and process until the mixture is blended. Add this mixture to a mixing bowl.

Dice the dates and remaining banana and add those to the mixture. Gradually mix in the flour until everything is evenly mixed.

Cut the mixture in half, make two loaves about an inch and a half (3 cm) high and dehydrate at 8 hours, turning over once halfway through.

Really Chocolate Pudding

Serves 2.

1/2 cup of chocolate powder (crushed cacao beans or nibs)

1 avocado, stoned and peeled

1/2 cup of carob powder

10 dates, stoned and soaked

2 tablespoons of raw agave nectar

Blend all ingredients together. If too bitter, add more agave nectar. Serve scooped or piped into a dish.

Sticky Hazelnut Clusters

Makes about 16 balls.

8 dates, soaked and stoned
1/2 cup of dried baby figs
2 cups of hazelnuts
2 tablespoons of raw agave nectar
1/2 cup of chocolate powder (crushed cacao beans or nibs)
Pinch of Celtic sea salt or Himalayan pink rock salt

Put the hazels into a food processor and process until broken, not powdery. Put them into a mixing bowl.

Put all the remaining ingredients into the food processor and process until the mixture starts to form a ball.

Take small sections of the mixture and roll into balls.

You can eat them as they are, or put them into a dehydrator for about 4 hours to solidify.

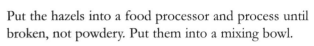

Everso Chocolate Cheezecake

Serves 8, but only if you're good.

Base

2 cups of hazelnuts

20 dates, stoned and soaked 2-24 hours

1 dessertspoon of chocolate powder (crushed cacao beans or nibs)

Middle

4 bananas, peeled, chopped and frozen for 24-48 hours

1/2 a vanilla pod

1 mango, stoned and peeled

1 tablespoon of carob powder

Topping

1 portion of **Really Chocolate Pudding** (see page 164)

1 portion of **Cashew Créme** (see page 196)

15 white grapes

1 physalis (gooseberry)

1 passion fruit

To make the base

Process the hazels, dates and chocolate powder in the food processor until smoothly blended together. Put this mixture into a loose-bottomed round tin (about 6-8 inches). Put this into the freezer while making the next layer.

To make the middle

Add the bananas, seeds from the vanilla pod and mango to the food processor. Process this until the mixture becomes white and creamy. Add the carob powder and process just enough to blend this in. Add this layer into the tin, on top of the hazelnut base, and spread it out evenly. Place it back in the freezer.

To complete

After at least 2 hours, remove the two-layers of cheezecake from the tin, and place on a serving plate. Add **Really Chocolate Pudding** to a piping bag and pipe a design on top. Clean the piping bag, then pipe with **Cashew Créme**. Add the grapes, passion fruit and physalis or other fruit in season.

Charlotte Rousse's Beetroot Mousse

This stunning savoury dish can be served as a starter or as an accompaniment to a main course.
Serves 2.

1 cup of fresh beetroot

1 small red onion

4 halves of sundried tomatoes, soaked 8-24 hours

3/4 cup of dry pine kernels

A squeeze of lemon juice

10 rosemary leaves

1 dessertspoon of chocolate powder (crushed cacao beans or nibs)

1/2 teaspoon of mustard powder

Dice the beetroot and onion, then add everything to a Vita-Mix or hand blender. Blend until completely homogenised. If you're doing this with a hand blender, it may help to start it all off in a food processor, and then finish with the hand blender.

Add the mixture to two small moulds, lined with cling film (Saran wrap) and turn out immediately or place in the fridge to set for a while. Decorate with any left over ingredients. We use a peeling of beetroot, some onion rings and some pine nuts.

It's the tomatoes that make this into a mousse, so if you're experimenting with other flavours, keep the tomatoes!

Chili con Cacao

This is a really intense meal, adjust the cayenne content according to your taste! Serves 4.

2 cloves of garlic

2 ripe medium tomatoes

1 cup of basil, loosely packed

10 rosemary leaves

6 sundried tomatoes

A squeeze of lemon

1 heaped teaspoon of cayenne powder

4 Peruvian dried olives, soaked 30 minutes

2 tablespoons of chocolate powder (crushed cacao beans or nibs)

1/2 red pepper

1/2 cup of dried mixed mushrooms

1/4 cup of olive oil

4 courgettes

Finely chop the garlic and rosemary. Dice the tomatoes and peppers. Slice the olives, and discard the stones. Add all the ingredients except the oil and courgettes to the food processor. If possible, crush the mushrooms in your hands before adding them. Process until the mixture is even and still chunky. Leave for 10 minutes for the mushrooms to expand and soak up some of the juice. Stir in the olive oil by hand.

Peel the courgettes and grate them. Pat with kitchen paper if they aren't very dry. Divide them into four, and place them on a plate, using a round mould. Dent the top slightly so the chili can fit into it.

Top the courgettes with equal amounts of chili and serve. For a special treat, serve with **Chocolate Tortillas**!

Chocolate Tortillas

These are slightly spicy, slightly chocolatey, and oh so versatile. We stuff them with Non-Fried Beans (recipe to follow), Chili con Cacao, our Sour Cream (recipe to follow), and marinated peppers. Serve them with guacamole, sunflower sprouts, slices of lime on a bed of spring onions. Makes 6 tortillas.

Corn freshly stripped from 2 cobs

1/2 cup of dry golden flax seeds

1/4 avocado

1/2 cup of sunflower seeds, dry

4 spring onions

2 cloves of garlic

1/4 teaspoon of Celtic sea salt or Himalayan pink rock salt

1 teaspoon of cumin powder

1/2 teaspoon of cayenne powder

1 dessertspoon of paprika

1 dessertspoon of chocolate powder (crushed cacao beans or nibs)

2 squeezes of lime juice

Grind the flax seeds into a fine powder using a spice mill. Finely chop the garlic. Chop the spring onions. Add all the ingredients to the food processor, and blend until smooth. The dough should be thick and sticky.

Place six equal amounts on Teflex sheets, flatten out into circles and dehydrate for about four hours. Turn the tortillas over, remove the Teflex sheets so air can circulate more and dehydrate for a further one or two hours.

Non-Fried Beans

This recipe goes really well with the tortillas, so even though it doesn't have chocolate in it, we've included it here. This tastes just like refried beans. Serves 6 when put in tortillas with the other ingredients.

2 cups of dry sunflower seeds

1/2 cup of olive oil

1 dessertspoon of paprika

1/4 red pepper

1 teaspoon of cumin seed

1/4 cup of salty water from Italian olives (or water with / teaspoon of Celtic sea salt or Himalayan pink rock salt in it)

1 dessertspoon of raw tahini

1 spring onion (green onion)

Chop the spring onion and pepper. Put all the ingredients in the food processor. Process until smooth and spreadable, which may take a few minutes. Warm this in your dehydrator for about half an hour before serving.

Sour Cream

This recipe goes really well with the tortillas, so even though it doesn't have chocolate in it, we've included it here. It tastes just like real sour cream, but it's so much better for you! Serves 6 when put in tortillas with the other ingredients. Keeps well in the fridge for a few weeks, so you can make a big batch.

2 cups of cashew nuts, soaked 2 hours

1/2 lemon

1/2 cup of celery juice or water (not the nut soak water)

1/2 teaspoon of Celtic sea salt or Himalayan pink rock salt

Juice the lemon, discard the pulp and skin. Add all the ingredients to a Vita-Mix or other high-powered blender. Blend until very smooth. Put in the fridge for at least an hour before serving.

Tortilla Chips

You can just use the tortilla recipe for this, and cut them differently, but we find that this slightly modified recipe works best. It's amazing how chocolate and spices go so well together. We love these with salsa and guacamole with some olives on the side. Makes 30-40 chips, depending on size.

Corn freshly stripped from 2 cobs

1/2 cup of dry golden flax seeds

1/4 avocado

1/2 cup sunflower seeds, dry

1 clove of garlic

1/4 teaspoon of Celtic sea salt

1 teaspoon of cumin powder

1 dessertspoon of paprika

2 dessertspoons of chocolate powder
   (crushed cacao beans or nibs)

2 squeezes of lime juice

To serve

1 teaspoon of Celtic sea salt

1/2 teaspooon ground coriander

Grind the flax seeds into a fine powder using a spice mill or Vita-Mix dry jug. Finely chop the garlic. Add all the ingredients (except the serving ingredients) to the food processor, and blend until smooth. The dough should be thick and sticky.

Put the dough onto a couple of Teflex sheets. Cover with cling film (Saran wrap), and roll out with a rolling pin until about 4mm thin. Remove the cling film and dehydrate for about 4 hours.

Turn the half-ready mixture onto dehydrator trays without the Teflex sheets, and score triangular chip-like shapes into them. Dehydrate for a further 4-6 hours, until crisp.

Grind the coriander and salt until fine, then toss the chips in this. Serve with your favourite dips.

Pineapple Pockets

These are so juicy and yummy. You may find it hard to share these, but do try!! Makes 8-10 pockets.

1 pineapple
1/2 serving of **Dark Chocolate Sauce** (see page 140)

Slice the pineapple into rings about 1.5 cm thick. Cut the edges off — We use a biscuit cutter to make them all the same. Gently slice into the centre of each slice, so you create a pocket.

Put a dollop of sauce into the centre of each pocket. Close the pocket and add to a dehydrator. Dehydrate for 4-6 hours, turning once.

Serve these as they are, still warm from the dehydrator, perhaps with one of our delicious ice creams.

The Golden Ticket

Just like Charlie Bucket, you can have your very own golden ticket — and you can eat it, too! Makes 2 big tickets.

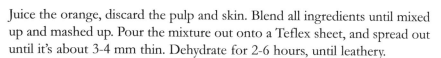

2 cups of pineapple

1 tablespoon of ionic angstrom gold

1 orange

1 dessertspoon of chocolate powder (crushed cacao beans or nibs)

Juice the orange, discard the pulp and skin. Blend all ingredients until mixed up and mashed up. Pour the mixture out onto a Teflex sheet, and spread out until it's about 3-4 mm thin. Dehydrate for 2-6 hours, until leathery.

Cut into two to make tickets, then dress up as Charlie and Willy and let the fun begin in your very own Wonka way!

Menage à Quatre

What are we suggesting here? Maybe not what you think. Yes four in a bed, but they're Charlie's grandparents. See — all very innocent. Bless them, they're old wrinkly prunes, but they still have smiles on their faces! So say hello to Grandma Josephine, Grandpa Joe, Grandma Georgina and Grandpa George. And then eat them. Ahem. Sorry. Serves 1.

6 prunes, soaked at least overnight, in plenty of water (they're thirsty!)

1/2 cup of macadamia nuts

1 teaspoon of maca

1 teaspoon of chocolate powder (crushed cacao beans or nibs)

1 tablespoon of soak water from the prunes

Raisins, apple and citrus peel to decorate

Skin and stone two of the prunes, and add to a food processor. Put the macadamias, maca, chocolate powder and prune juice in there, too. Process until blended, yet still crunchy.

Put this on a plate and shape into a rectangle. This will be the lovely cozy bed for the grandparents. Decorate the bed with raisins.

Gently stone the remaining four prunes, and then lay them on their bed. Create faces for them all out of citrus peel. Make hair for the Grandmas, they may be old, but they still want to look good for the Grandpas!

Chocolate Pizza

This tastes like no other pizza you've ever known! Serves 8, if giving one slice each.

Dough

1 cup of dry oat groats

1 cup of dry cashew nuts

1 teaspoon of dry golden flaxseed

15 dried apricots, soaked 4-6 hours

Topping

1 large strawberry

1 apple

4 physalis (gooseberries)

4 grapes

1 portion of **Dark Chocolate Sauce** (see page 140)

To make the dough

Put 8 cashews to one side. Grind the remaining cashews, flax and oat groats into a fine "flour", using a Nutri-Bullet, Vita-Mix dry jug or a coffee mill. Transfer to a food processor, saving about a tablespoon for rolling the dough out. Switch the food processor on, and drop the apricots down the chute. As the apricots are blended, a dough-like consistency will form. If it doesn't, add some of the soak water from the apricots. Once it's formed into a ball, switch the machine off and remove the dough from the bowl.

Place some flour onto a chopping board. Put the dough on this, and then add some more flour onto the dough. Start to flatten and roll the dough, as you would any other dough until it's about seven inches round. Once rolled, place it on a dehydrator tray, and dehydrate for 4-6 hours, turning once.

Once dehydrated (firm, but not crisp), remove the base from the tray and place on a serving plate.

To assemble

Pour the chocolate sauce onto the base. Slice the strawberry into eight pieces and arrange in a circle. Cut the grapes and physalis into halves and place these on the pizza. Put the cashews in the middle. Grate some apple over the top of all of this.

Individual Deep Pecan Pies

Ah, these are so yummy. They're big, too, so have one as a whole meal! Serves 6.

1 cup of dry oat groats

1 cup of dry pecan nuts

1 teaspoon of golden flax seed

40 dried apricots, soaked for 8-24 hours

4 tablespoons of chocolate powder (crushed cacao beans or nibs)

30 extra pecans

6 teaspoons of raw agave nectar

Grind the pecans, flax and oat groats into a fine "flour", using a Nutri-Bullet, Vita-Mix dry jug or in a coffee mill. Transfer to a food processor, saving about a tablespoon for rolling the dough out. Switch the food processor on, and drop 15 of the apricots down the chute. As the apricots are blended, a dough-like consistency will form. If it doesn't, add some of the soak water from the apricots. Once it's formed into a ball, switch the machine off and remove the dough from the bowl.

Place some flour onto a chopping board. Put the dough on this, and then add some more flour onto the dough. Start to flatten and roll the dough, as you would any other dough. Make it about a quarter of an inch thick. Once rolled, cut six circles out which are big enough to fill deep, three or four inch pie dishes. Add cling film (Saran wrap) to the dishes. Press the pastry into the pie dishes, and cut the edges off. Flute the edges.

Place these pies in a dehydrator for two hours. The pastry will harden slightly. Carefully remove the pastry from the trays, by turning them upside down. Remove the cling film. Removing them like this enables more warm air to reach the underside of the pastry, and crisps it up. Put the formed shells back on a dehydrator tray and dehydrate for two more hours.

When your pastry shells are ready, remove them from the dehydrator and put them to one side.

Using a hand blender, mix the remaining apricots with the chocolate powder. Transfer equal amounts of that to each pastry shell. Top with five pecans each. Drizzle over a teaspoon of agave nectar on each pie. Dehydrate these for a further hour or two to warm through. Serve with some gorgeous ice cream!

Chocolate Tarts

The Queen of Hearts, she made some tarts, but didn't want them strawberry-red, so painted them chocolate-brown instead. Makes 12.

1 cup of dry oat groats
1 cup of dry almonds
1 teaspoon of golden flax seed
15 dried apricots, soaked for 4-6 hours
1 serving of **Dark Chocolate Sauce** (see page 140)

Grind the almonds, flax and oat groats into a fine "flour", using a Vita-Mix dry jug or in a coffee mill. Transfer to a food processor, saving about one tablespoon for rolling the dough out. Switch the food processor on, and drop 15 of the apricots down the chute. As the apricots are blended, a dough-like consistency will form. If it doesn't, add some of the soak water from the apricots. Once it's formed into a ball, switch the machine off and remove the dough from the bowl.

Place some flour onto a chopping board. Put the dough on this, and then add some more flour onto the dough. Start to flatten and roll the dough, as you would any other dough. Make it about 4mm thick. Once rolled, cut twelve circles out with a biscuit cutter. Add cling film (Saran wrap) to a tart/bun tray. Place the pastry into the tray.

Place this in a dehydrator for 2 hours. The pastry will harden slightly. Carefully remove the pastries from the dish and remove the cling film. Removing them like this enables more warm air to reach the underside of the pastry, and crisps it up. Put the pastries back on a dehydrator tray and dehydrate for one more hour.

When your pastry shells are ready, remove them from the dehydrator and pour equal amounts of **Dark Chocolate Sauce** into them.

Kumquats Stuffed with Chocolate Hazelnuts

These make great little aperitifs. They are quite strong in flavour, so nibble delicately! Makes 24.

1 cup of raisins, soaked

1/2 a cup of walnuts, soaked

Crushed hazelnuts, dry

1/2 a cup of chocolate powder (crushed cacao beans or nibs)

12 kumquats

Blend the raisins and walnuts until the mixture is a mouldable consistency. Add the chocolate powder. Roll into oblong balls and then roll onto the crushed hazelnuts until they're covered.

Cut each kumquat in half, and scoop or cut out the bitter flesh. Place an oblong ball into each kumquat half. Arrange on a plate and serve.

Choco-Nut Spread

We love to serve this with apple wedges! You can also spread it on sweet potatoes, sandwich it between bananas, or spread it on someone you love! This is another recipe we keep as a staple in our fridges.

1 cup of raw almond butter

2 dessertspoons of chocolate powder (crushed cacao beans or nibs)

1/4 cup of raw agave nectar

Mix all ingredients together with a fork and you're ready to paint the town brown!

Choccie Yum-Yums

These are the sweetest little sweeties that we make. Full of goodness, taste and love. Makes about 40 yum-yums.

1 cup of dry almonds

Skin of 1 kumquat, or 1 dessertspoon of orange peel

25 dates, stoned

1 serving of **Choco-Nut Spread** (see page 189)

1/4 cup of raw agave nectar

1 teaspoon of mixed spice

Finely shred the kumquat skin. Add all ingredients to a food processor and process until the mixture forms a ball. If the mixture doesn't look like it's going to stick together, add more agave nectar.

Turn the mixture out onto a chopping board, and roll out to an 8 mm thick square with a rolling pin. It won't need any "flour" as the agave nectar stops the mixture from sticking. Cut into 2 cm squares and pile on a plate. These are delicious as they are, and also great when put in the fridge or freezer for a while.

Rich Chocolate Fruit Sorbet

This has a really intense flavour, and will give you a chocolate kick up the bottom unlike any other chocolate sorbet does! Serves 4.

1/2 cup of chocolate powder (crushed cacao beans or nibs)

1/2 cup of water

1/2 cup of agave nectar

1/2 a vanilla pod

2 cups of frozen strawberries and/or raspberries

Thaw the fruit for five minutes to make it easier to blend. Split the vanilla down the middle and scrape the seeds into the blender. Discard the skin, or add to a bottle of agave nectar to make it vanilla flavoured!

Add all the other ingredients to the blender and blend until smooth. Put in the freezer until you need it. I decorate this with a touch of flaked coconut.

Crying in the Chapple Pie

Crust

1.5 cups of sunflower seeds

1 cup of raisins

Half an orange

1 thin slice of lemon, including the skin (discard any pips)

2 tablespoons of chocolate powder (crushed cacao beans or nibs)

Filling

4 large apples, peeled and cored

3/4 cup of agave nectar

1 dessertspoon of cinnamon powder

Pinch of cloves powder

1/2 lemon

Decoration

Dried coconut, finely shredded

Thin slices of apple

Ice cream (use one from this book!)

Raw agave nectar

Cinnamon powder

To make the crust

Juice the orange and discard the skin and pulp. Place all the crust ingredients in a food processor until finely ground and the mixture sticks together.

Press the mixture into an eight inch pie dish. Form the crust, pushing it right up to the edges.

To make the filling

Juice the lemon. Process half the apples for about a minute in the food processor. Add the rest of the apples and all the other filling ingredients. Process again until everything's mixed and chopped into small pieces, but not mushed (you process the apples in two stages to create texture).

Put this mixture into a sieve to strain the excess juice off. Keep this juice.

Put the mixture into the pie crust and smooth it out. It should come to just below the pie crust. Put this pie into the fridge or freezer to set for about an hour.

Hint: Line the dish with cling film (Saran wrap), and put cling film on top of the crust mix, too. This makes it easier to flatten out evenly, and it doesn't stick to the tin when you remove the pie.

To complete

Add thin slices of apple and the other decoration ingredients and serve. If you like, spoon over some of the left over liquid from the apple mixture or use it in another recipe.

Little Fudge Cakes

Makes about 24 little cakes. Make sure you share them!

2 dessertspoons of raw tahini

2.5 cups of dry almonds

2 tablespoons of raw agave nectar or yacon root syrup

5 dates, stoned

1 dessertpoon of chocolate powder (crushed cacao beans or nibs)

2 tablespoons of dried, finely shredded coconut

1 dessertspoon of coconut oil/butter

Pinch of nutmeg

Pinch of cinnamon

1 dessertspoon of cold-pressed flax oil

1 dessertspoon of cold-pressed olive oil

1/4 teaspoon of Celtic sea salt or Himalayan pink rock salt

Mill two cups of almonds into a "flour" using the Vita-Mix dry jug or a coffee mill. Chop the dates. Add all the ingredients to a food processor and blend until it sticks together and still has bits in it. Place the mixture on a shallow tray, flatten it out, cut into squares and serve or store in the fridge.

Hint: Line the tin with cling film (Saran wrap), and put cling film on top of the cake mix, too. This makes it easier to flatten out evenly, and it doesn't stick to the tin when you remove the cakes.

Almond Mylk

Yes, we know there's no chocolate in here (though if you add a spoonful of it and some agave or yacon syrup, you'll get a great chocolate mylk!). However, we use almond mylk in several recipes, so you need to know how to make it. It's easy and will last for 3 days in the fridge. Just shake it before use. Add a couple of drops of angstrom/ionic silver to prolong the shelf life. Makes about 1 litre.

2 cups of almonds, soaked in water overnight

1 litre of your preferred water

Raw agave nectar or yacon root syrup (optional)

Put the almonds in a blender and add half the water. Blend until the almonds are pulverised. Pour this mixture into a large clean jug, through a fine strain (Shazzie uses a clean pop-sock!).

Put the almond meal back into the blender and pour the remaining water into the blender. Blend and strain as before. Add the agave nectar if you wish.

You can discard the leftover meal or use it as a pie base in another recipe.

Pour the mylk into clean jars and seal them.

Cashew Créme

Makes 1 serving, to add to any of the sweet recipes in this book.

2 cups of dry cashew nuts

1 cup of young coconut water (or orange juice as a substitute)

1 dessertspoon of raw agave nectar or yacon root syrup

2 inches of fresh vanilla pod

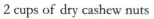

Blend all the ingredients using either a hand blender or a Nutri-Bullet. Strain through a nut milk bag if you like, to remove any vanilla parts. To make more like double cream, use more nuts or less liquid. If your blender isn't very strong, you may wish to just use the vanilla seeds from inside the pod.

Ice Cream Floats

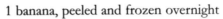

Ahhh. Remember those lovely fizzy, cold, creamy dreamy drinks of yesteryear? Well, we have a choccie one for you to go bonkers on! Serves 2.

1 pint of good carbonated water

Water from 1 young coconut

1 tablespoon of raw agave nectar

1/2 lemon

Pinch of nutmeg

1 banana, peeled and frozen overnight

1 dessertspoon of chocolate powder (crushed cacao beans or nibs)

1 teaspoon of **Dark Chocolate Sauce** (optional)

Process the banana and chocolate powder as you would for the **Mint Chocolate Chip Ice Cream** recipe (see page 158). Juice the lemon, discarding the pulp and skin. In a blender, blend the coconut water, agave nectar and lemon juice together. Pour the fizzy water into the blender and mix this in with a spoon (do not blend it — It'll fizz up all over the place). Pour this into long, cool glasses and add equal amounts of banana ice cream on top. Add some nutmeg, drizzle over the chocolate sauce, and serve with a long spoon, straw and a lovely smile.

Orange Chollies

You need some lolly moulds for this, but if you don't have any, you can pour the mixture into ice cube trays and make finger-lollies. Makes 6 chollies.

2 large oranges

1 tablespoon of chocolate powder (crushed cacao beans or nibs)

1 dessertspoon of coconut oil/butter

Pinch of paprika

10 dates, stoned

Juice the oranges and discard the skins and pulp. Blend all the ingredients thoroughly, pour into the lolly moulds and freeze.

Appendices

"Too much of a good thing is
simply WONDERFUL!!!"
— Deborah Fox-Rothschild

Appendix A: Chocolate For The Skin

Cacao oil/butter (otherwise known as cocoa butter or cocoa oil) possesses the useful qualities of having an aphrodisiac smell, high antioxidant levels, skin protective qualities, a melt point at just below the temperature of the human body and resistance to rancidity.

The oil/butter of cacao is a treat for our sense of smell. It is agreeable to our tastes and highly nutritious. It has been used as a substitute for, or an alternative to, cod-liver oil, and as an article of diet during the last days of pregnancy. It works great on the lips and makes one feel beautifully chocolatey! Due to its high antioxidant level, it has been used as a primary ingredient in suntan lotions for many years. It has also been employed in the formation of suppositories and pessaries for rectal, vaginal and other applications. It is in many preparations for rough or chafed skin, chapped lips, sore nipples, lotions, various cosmetics and soaps.

On the Composition of Cacao Butter — Kingzett announced in 1877 the isolation of two fatty acids; one was named theobromic acid, and was stated to have the formula $C_{64}H_{128}O_2$. Vander Becke in 1880 endeavoured to prepare the latter, but without success. The subject was investigated by M. C. Traub, who examined five samples of oil of theobroma, two of which he himself had prepared. After saponification, the acids were ascertained to be completely precipitated by magnesium acetate. By repeated fractional precipitation it was proven that the oil consists of the glyceryl esters of oleic, lauric, palmitic, stearic and arachic acids. The solid consistency of the oil and its low melting point are most likely due to the peculiar proportions in which these compounds are combined resembling in this respect the behaviour of certain metals (reference: **Archiv d. Phar.**, Jan., 1883, p. 19-23).

Appendix B: The Chocolate Religion

You'll be glad to know that we do have a religion for you to join: the chocolate religion! It is 100% non-denominational. Anyone is welcome as long as they love chocolate! This religion is founded on two principles: absolute silliness and the best day ever!

We do actually have one requirement, that you read and study the chocolate bible on a regular basis: **Charlie and the Chocolate Factory** by Roald Dahl. We are looking to get a **Charlie and the Chocolate Factory** into every hotel room in the world.

We recommend using the Mayan calendar because it is so cool and weird... plus it was made by the Mayans who loved chocolate!

We founded The Chocolate Religion on July 14th, 2003. In the Dreamspell Mayan calendar this date is Red Planetary Moon Year, Cosmic moon, 18th day (Kin 142: White Crystal Wind.) You are welcome to celebrate the Chocolate New Year of July 14th annually with us!

We have recently nominated a Chocolate Pope. Since no one else has stepped forward, we have chosen David Wolfe as Chocolate Pope Avocado Cacao I.

We have also nominated Amsterdam as the Chocolate Capital of the World because Amsterdam is the funniest, zaniest place ever!

We are currently conducting Chocolate Revivals in cities all over the world. We are calling our chocolate parties *Raw Cacao Dance Parties*. Please check www.davidwolfe.com for a *Raw Cacao Dance Party* event in your area.

Shazzie and David in Amsterdam, 2003, when they founded The Chocolate Religion. This unedited photo came as a result of a week on cacao, maca and blue-green algae. Oh, the possibilities.

Appendix C: Finding The Best Chocolate

"Like wine, chocolate is an agricultural product that goes through enhancing transformations, which can turn blah into acceptable. What no amount of processing can do is create greatness without great raw material. Like wine grapes, most of the world's cacao beans are workhorse types, useful for providing bulk, but unable to deliver more than a basic chocolate taste. Only a small percentage can express the enormous range of flavours that inspires poetic analogies." — **Money** magazine, February 9, 2004

"A little of what you fancy does you good." — Folk wisdom

Recommendations for Purchasing Processed Chocolate

When purchasing processed chocolate, one should look to see that it meets some, or all, of the following criteria:

• Organic

• No dairy

• No genetically modified soy lecithin (the label must say "organic" or non-GMO soy lecithin)

• 70%+ cacao content. (It is legal to call 41% cacao content a dark chocolate which allows manufacturers room to hide defects and poor quality beans).

• "Single Origin" — chocolate made with cacao beans from a particular country or area.

• "Single Estate" — chocolate made with cacao beans from a single estate. Sometimes called "Estate Grown" or "Terroir style" meaning, "the taste of the place."

• "Single Variety" — chocolate made exclusively from one particular cacao bean type (ie. *Criollo*)

Processed Chocolate Tasting

Good processed chocolate melts slowly in your mouth, delivering a blend of flowers, fruit, spice, nuts, with undertones of good tobacco. If you taste acids, grass, mold, rubber, smoke, and/or straw, you know there were troubles in growing, processing, and/or storage.

How To Order Cacao Beans and Unique Chocolate Products

The products listed below are raw and organic (free of pesticides and chemical fertlizers). Beware of non-organic cacao beans (nibs). In the U.S. it is a law and common practice to fumigate cacao being imported into the country. Essentially, non-organic cacao has been fumigated. We strongly promote organic agriculture. Also, our particular organic cacao beans (nibs) have low microbe counts on the skin, therefore you can eat the skin and avoid peeling.

Available Chocolate Alchemy Products

Chocolate Books

Naked Chocolate
Charlie and the Chocolate Factory by Roald Dahl

Food Products

Sacred Chocolate (stone-ground superhero chocolate bars)

Amazonian peanuts (wild)

Bee pollen

Blue-green algae (Klamath Lake E3 Live)

Cacao beans (raw, peeled, organic, heirloom)

Cacao butter (raw, organic, heirloom)

Cacao nibs (raw, peeled, organic, heirloom)

Cacao paste (raw, stone-ground, organic, heirloom)

Carob powder

Cashews (raw)

Cayenne pepper

Chia seeds

Chlorella

Figs (dried)

Flax seeds

Goji berries

Hemp seeds

Immortal Machine (superfood formula)

Incan berries

Kelp (powdered)

Maca powder

Marine phytoplankton

Mesquite powder

NoniLand honey

NoniLand noni powder

NoniLand superfood formula

Olives

Purple corn

Royal Jelly

Spirulina

Tocotrienols (also known as tocos) — mechanically separated rice bran

Vanilla beans

Oils

Cacao butter (raw)
Coconut butter
Coconut oil
Hempseed oil
Olive oil

Salts

Sea salt (Celtic grey mineral,
   Hawaiian, New Zealand)
Himalayan pink rock salt

Tea Ingredients

Pau d'Arco
Cat's Claw
Chancapiedra
Chuchuhuasi
Gynostemma

Supplements

Angstrom Calcium
Angstrom Gold
MegaHydrate (antioxidants)
MSM powder (plant-derived
   methyl-sulphonyl-methane)

Appliances

Nut milk bags
Dehydrators
Juicers
Blenders including the Nutri-Bullet
   and/or Vita-Mix
Coffee grinder
Spice mill
Food processor

All these chocolate alchemy products, as well as certified organic, raw cacao products are sold in the **United States** by:

Longevity Warehouse
www.LongevityWarehouse.com

And in the **United Kingdom** by:

Detox Your World (Rawcreation Ltd)
PO Box 223
Belton
Great Yarmouth
NR31 9WX
www.detoxyourworld.com | sales@detoxyourworld.com
08700 113 119

Index

"Just a moment," he said. "Now we shall witness an undeniable proof of the infinite power of God. … The boy who had helped him with the mass brought him a cup of thick and steaming chocolate, which he drank without pausing to breathe. Then he wiped his lips with a handkerchief that he drew from his sleeve, extended his arms, and closed his eyes. Thereupon Father Nicanor rose six inches above the level of the ground. It was a convincing measure. He went among the houses for several days repeating the demonstration of levitation by means of chocolate while the acolyte collected so much money in a bag that in less than a month he began the construction of the church. No one doubted the divine origin of the demonstration except Jose."

— Gabriel García Márquez (from *One Hundred Years of Solitude*)

noni, 115, 116
noradrenalin, 45, 61, 63
norepinephrine, 45, 61
Norwegians, 2
nut, 14, 27, 57, 63, 107, 108, 111, 154, 174, 196
nut milk bag, 154, 196
nutmeg, 75, 80, 86, 87, 136, 148, 150, 194, 197
Nutri-Bullet, 124, 125, 135, 136, 137, 138, 140, 154, 182, 184, 196, 204

O

oat groats, 138, 156, 157, 162, 163, 182, 184, 186
Oaxaca, 74, 75, 77, 80, 81
obesity, 65, 88
octli, 105
oil, 5, 11, 13, 14, 19, 45, 61, 78, 90, 92, 96, 108, 113, 114, 115, 118, 119, 131, 140, 143, 146, 149, 154, 155, 158, 170, 174, 194, 197, 200, 204, 243, 245
oleic acid, 36, 40
olive, 115, 170, 174, 194
olive oil, 115, 170, 174, 194
Olmecs, 15
omega 3 fatty acid, 40, 45
omega 6 fatty acid, 40, 115
onion, 113, 169, 174
ORAC level, 54, 55
orange, 10, 12, 73, 96, 113, 136, 150, 151, 161, 179, 190, 192, 193, 196
Orange Chollies, 197
orator, 71
orchid, 110
organic, 6, 11, 30, 56, 64, 80, 96, 98, 99, 103, 117, 127, 202, 203, 204, 245, 246
organic food, 103
Orinoco river, 11, 15
Other Books & Projects by David Wolfe, 244
Other Books & Projects by Shazzie, 242
Other Old and New Friends of Cacao, 111
Ott, Jonathan, 31, 42, 73, 74, 75, 78, 88
Overcoming Chocolate Addictions, 92
oxalic acid, 36
oxidation, 53, 121
oxygen, 52, 95, 121

P

Pacal Votan, 82, 83
Pacific Ocean, 18, 115
Palenque, 82

palmitic (acid), 40, 200
palmitic acid, 36
Panama, 12, 54
pantothenic acid, 36, 38, 42
papain, 116
papaya, 102, 115, 116, 134
Papaya Cheezes, 134
paprika, 173, 174, 176, 197
paradise, 17, 99
parrots, 10
Passiflora spp., 64, 104, 116
passion fruit, 102, 116, 166
pataxte, 14
p-coumaric acid, 36, 39
PEA, 34, 60, 61, 70, 92, 112
peanuts, 110
pecans, 129, 150, 184
pectin, 36
penis, 69
pentose, 36
peppermint, 154
peptides, 27
peroxidase, 36
Persian, 114
persimmon, 127
Peru, 8, 13, 109, 119
pesticide, 6, 97
pesticide-free technique, 97
Peter, Daniel, 20
peyote, 76
pH, 5, 42
Pharmacotheon, 73
phenylalanine, 37, 39, 73, 106
phenylethylamine, 34, 37, 59, 60, 70, 71, 73, 76, 88, 89, 92, 93, 112
phospholipids, 37, 41
phosphorus, 37, 38, 106, 110
Photo Credits, 241
phycocyanin, 112
physalis, 127, 166, 182
Physiologie de Gout, 86
Phytophthora spp., 97
phytosterols, 41, 106, 114
pigment, 27, 42, 112
Pimienta dioica, 104
pine kernels, 169
pineapple, 116, 178, 179
Pineapple Pockets, 178

A Secret History of Chocolate

by David Wolfe, December 2003

"There's more to life than chocolate, but not right now."
— Anonymous

Over eons of astrology
Transformations of geology
Here still, right now
Is this black seed — cacao.

The seed of a fruit of a sacred tree
A gentle, jungle species under the vast canopy.

The Food of the Gods
Hidden there in hardened fruit pods.

Of all the jungle — rain forest
You have surpassed the best.

Twelve hundred elements of flavour
And every one to savour.

So silly, have you heard?
The answer is absurd!

Seed-food of a race long gone
Melted through cooking — withdrawn.

Now resurrected, back for more
Cacao has more surprises in store.

Inside the seeds of these fruits high above
Are the chemicals of bliss, focus — love.

Carrying forth nobility,
A lost Mayan beauty.

Cracked, eaten, dipped in honey
Chocolate is an edible money!

Boosts, potentiates, exposes
Mixed with cherimoyas, roses
Adds style, fashion
To the fruits of passion.

It is a food of prosperity — without hoarding
Yet useless to the boring.

Subtle, eclectic.
It transforms the mundane
To the psychedelic.

Entheogenic, yet mild,
Still growing wild,
Where tribes had been
With psilocybin.
Cacao can converse
And travel the universe.

Cacao is from some mystical realm
And it's just enough to overwhelm
The daily routine, the chain of time
Slowing the rhythm, showing a rhyme.

The spirit of the thing:
Some ancient, Mayan king
Of legends and tales
Who, over oceans sailed,
A being empires hailed.

Male, delicate,
Lean, effeminate,
Dark nails, hands strong,
Limbs smooth and long.

From the waist up to the chest
In a vanilla, v-cut, vest
Embroidered, broad-wide
Opened up the sides.

Dark, brown, tan,
Eyes glowing — and:

Hair braided,
Muscles serrated,
Jewelry jaded,
Regal, fated
To alter the course of history
By some fantastic mystery.

Who had, through remarkable demur,
Been tricked by the allure
Of the Faustian game
Fire, heat, flame
And the devil's signed name.

Tossed into milk, imprisoned, cursed
To create an insatiable thirst.
Dissolved, tricked, corroded
And then through boat-ships unloaded
As candy and confections.
Seduced, inducing infections.

And yet, now we discover,
Cacao cannot be made the miser,
And chocolate has become a little wiser.

Cacao, you see,
Is a student, sent
Learning while others came and went.

Chocolate studies all — with a twist:
The cacao god is an alchemist.

A new strategy emerges
Where past and future diverges
We never knew,
Until now,
Lost in time somehow,
The secret law:
Chocolate must be eaten raw.

Inscribed in ancient stone, clay, pottery.
It makes you the winner of the lottery;
The holder of the golden ticket,
And all you have to do is pick it,
Or it picks you
And you are created anew.

From the chocolate bean and vanilla inspiring
In comes a new era of literature, writing.

From somewhere deep inside this tree
Comes deeper, richer, poetry.

A seed that lowers appetite,
Makes you feel and look — just right
And always provides brilliant insight.

Depression healed, tempers calmed
Hearing the melody of hidden songs.

Exploding creativity,
Exciting nerve electricity,
Revealing synchronicity,
Giggling with eccentricity.

Radical,
Pharmacological,
Ecological,
Perfectly Illogical.

Chocolate is not to be cooked.
The obvious has been overlooked.

Consider…
A food that brings out your better half,
And causes little children to laugh.
That can save the planet
Before it's too late,
Because chocolate is already legal
In every state.

A new tale to an epic song,
A truth set right after so many wrongs.

The Cacao God has spoken
The curse-spell has now been broken.
Raw chocolate has found its hour
To conquer the ivory tower.

The Last Bits

"Eve left the garden of eden for chocolate."
— Anonymous

References Part I: Cacao

Legends of Cacao

Books

Time-Life Books' Myth And Mankind Series / Lost Realms of Gold: "South American Myth"; 1998, page 31.

Brenner, Joel Glenn. **The Emperors of Chocolate**, Broadway Books: New York, p. 64.

Coe, Sophie D. and Coe, Michael D. **The True History of Chocolate**. New York: Thames and Hudson, 1996.

Kilham, Chris. **Psyche Delicacies: Coffee, Chocolate, Chiles, Kava, and Cannabis, and Why They're Good For You**. Emmaus, PA: Rodale Press, 2001.

Lopez, Ruth. **Chocolate: The Nature of Indulgence**. New York: Harry N. Abrams, 2002.

Pendell, Dale. **Pharmako/Dynamis: Stimulating Plants, Potions, and Herbcraft**. Revised edition. Berkeley, CA: North Atlantic Books, 2010.

Presilla, Maricel E. **The New Taste of Chocolate: A Cultural and Natural History of Cacao with Recipes**. Berkeley, CA: Ten Speed Press, 2001.

Theobroma Cacao (The Chocolate Tree)

Books

Coe, Sophie D. and Coe, Michael D. **The True History of Chocolate**. New York: Thames and Hudson, 1996.

Dahl, Roald. **Charlie and the Chocolate Factory**. New York: Puffin Books, copyright 1964, 1998 edition.

Foster, Nelson and Cordell, Linda S. **Chilies to Chocolate: Food the Americas Gave the World**. Tucson, AZ: University of AZ Press, 1992.

Kilham, Chris. **Psyche Delicacies: Coffee, Chocolate, Chiles, Kava, and Cannabis, and Why They're Good For You**. Emmaus, PA: Rodale Press, 2001.

Lopez, Ruth. **Chocolate: The Nature of Indulgence**. New York: Harry N. Abrams, 2002.

McFadden, Christine and France, Christine. **Chocolate: Cooking with the World's Best Ingredient**. London: Hermes House, 1997.

Pendell, Dale. **Pharmako/Dynamis: Stimulating Plants, Potions, and Herbcraft**. Revised edition. Berkeley, CA: North Atlantic Books, 2010.

Presilla, Maricel E. **The New Taste of Chocolate: A Cultural and Natural History of Cacao with Recipes**. Berkeley, CA: Ten Speed Press, 2001.

Young, Allen M. **The Chocolate Tree: A Natural History of Cacao**. Washington, D.C.: Smithsonian Institution Press, 1994.

Articles

"The Republic of 'Gran Cacao'" (no author cited). **Slow Food Magazine**, April 2003, pgs 22-31.

Coe, Michael D. "In the Beginning was Kakaw." **Slow Food Magazine**, April 2003, pgs 40-43.

Motamayor JC, Lachenaud P, da Silva e Mota JW, Loor R, Kuhn DN, et al. (2008) "Geographic and Genetic Population Differentiation of the Amazonian Chocolate Tree (Theobroma cacao L)." **PLoS ONE** 3(10): e3311. doi:10.1371/journal.pone.0003311

A Brief History of Chocolate

Books

Coe, Sophie D. and Coe, Michael D. **The True History of Chocolate**. New York: Thames and Hudson, 1996.

Dahl, Roald. **Charlie and the Chocolate Factory**. New York: Puffin Books, copyright 1964, 1998 edition.

Foster, Nelson and Cordell, Linda S. **Chilies to Chocolate: Food the Americas Gave the World**. Tucson, AZ: University of AZ Press, 1992.

Kilham, Chris. **Psyche Delicacies: Coffee, Chocolate, Chiles, Kava, and Cannabis, and Why They're Good For You**. Emmaus, PA: Rodale Press, 2001.

Lopez, Ruth. **Chocolate: The Nature of Indulgence**. New York: Harry N. Abrams, 2002.

McFadden, Christine and France, Christine. **Chocolate: Cooking with the World's Best Ingredient**. London: Hermes House, 1997.

Pendell, Dale. **Pharmako/Dynamis: Stimulating Plants, Potions, and Herbcraft**. Revised edition. Berkeley, CA: North Atlantic Books, 2010.

Presilla, Maricel E. **The New Taste of Chocolate: A Cultural and Natural History of Cacao with Recipes**. Berkeley, CA: Ten Speed Press, 2001.

Young, Allen M. **The Chocolate Tree: A Natural History of Cacao**. Washington, D.C.: Smithsonian Institution Press, 1994.

Articles

"The Republic of 'Gran Cacao'" (no author cited): **Slow Food Magazine**, April 2003, pgs 22-31.

Coe, Michael D. "In the Beginning was Kakaw." **Slow Food Magazine**, April 2003, pgs 40-43.

Money Does Grow On Trees

Books

Coe, Sophie D. and Coe, Michael D. **The True History of Chocolate**. New York: Thames and Hudson, 1996.

Dahl, Roald. **Charlie and the Chocolate Factory**. New York: Puffin Books, copyright 1964, 1998 edition.

Foster, Nelson and Cordell, Linda S. **Chilies to Chocolate: Food the Americas Gave the World**. Tucson, AZ: University of AZ Press, 1992.

Kilham, Chris. **Psyche Delicacies: Coffee, Chocolate, Chiles, Kava, and Cannabis, and Why They're Good For You**. Emmaus, PA: Rodale Press, 2001.

Lopez, Ruth. **Chocolate: The Nature of Indulgence**. New York: Harry N. Abrams, 2002.

McFadden, Christine and France, Christine. **Chocolate: Cooking with the World's Best Ingredient**. London: Hermes House, 1997.

Pendell, Dale. **Pharmako/Dynamis: Stimulating Plants, Potions, and Herbcraft**. Revised edition. Berkeley, CA: North Atlantic Books, 2010.

Presilla, Maricel E. The **New Taste of Chocolate: A Cultural and Natural History of Cacao with Recipes**. Berkeley, CA: Ten Speed Press, 2001.

Young, Allen M. **The Chocolate Tree: A Natural History of Cacao**. Washington, D.C.: Smithsonian Institution Press, 1994.

Articles

"The Republic of 'Gran Cacao'" (no author cited): **Slow Food Magazine**, April 2003, pgs 22-31.

Coe, Michael D. "In the Beginning was Kakaw." **Slow Food Magazine**, April 2003, pgs 40-43.

Knight, I. "Chocolate and Cocoa: Health and Nutrition." **Blackwell Science**, 1999.

Zumbe, A. "Polyphenols in Cocoa: Are There Health Benefits?" **BNF Nutrition Bulletin**, volume 23, pp. 94-102, Spring 1998.

References Part II: Scientific Properties of Chocolate

Chemical Composition of Cacao

Books

Ashton, Dr. John and Ashton, Suzy. **A Chocolate A Day**. New York: Thomas Dunne Books, St. Martin's Press, 2001.

Coe, Sophie D. and Coe, Michael D. **The True History of Chocolate**. New York: Thames and Hudson, 1996.

Foster, Nelson and Cordell, Linda S. **Chilies to Chocolate: Food the Americas Gave the World**. Tucson, AZ: University of AZ Press, 1992.

Kilham, Chris. **Psyche Delicacies: Coffee, Chocolate, Chiles, Kava, and Cannabis, and Why They're Good For You**. Emmaus, PA: Rodale Press, 2001.

Lopez, Ruth. **Chocolate: The Nature of Indulgence**. New York: Harry N. Abrams, 2002.

Pendell, Dale. **Pharmako/Dynamis: Stimulating Plants, Potions, and Herbcraft**. Revised edition. Berkeley, CA: North Atlantic Books, 2010.

Presilla, Maricel E. **The New Taste of Chocolate: A Cultural and Natural History of Cacao with Recipes**. Berkeley, CA: Ten Speed Press, 2001.

Young, Allen M. **The Chocolate Tree: A Natural History of Cacao**. Washington, D.C.: Smithsonian Institution Press, 1994.

Articles

"The Republic of 'Gran Cacao'" (no author cited): **Slow Food Magazine**, April 2003, pgs 22-31.

Coe, Michael D. "In the Beginning was Kakaw." **Slow Food Magazine**, April 2003, pgs 40-43.

Clarkson, T.S., **Amer. Jour. Pharm.**, 1887, p. 277 (Cacao shells/skins research)

Web sites

www.uspharmacist.com "The Health Benefits of Dark Chocolate," George Nemecz, PhD (Vol. No. 29:02, posted 2/15/4)

www.rain-tree.com/db/theobroma-cacao-phytochem.htm (Dr. Duke's Phytochemical and Ethnobotanical Databases)

Magnesium

Books

Cousens, Gabriel, MD with Mark Mayell. **Depression-Free for Life**. New York: Harper Collins, 2001.

Jensen, Dr Bernard. **Dr. Jensen's Guide To Body Chemistry & Nutrition**. Los Angeles, CA: Keats Publishing, 2000.

Kervran, Professor C. Louis. **Biological Transmutations**. Asheville, NC: Happiness Press, 2003.

Ott, A. True, PhD. **Wellness Secrets For Life: An Owner's Manual For The Human Body**. Cedar City, UT: Cedar Mountain Publishing.

Antioxidants

Books

Kilham, Chris. **Psyche Delicacies: Coffee, Chocolate, Chiles, Kava, and Cannabis, and Why They're Good For You**. Emmaus, PA: Rodale Press, 2001.

Young, Allen M. **The Chocolate Tree: A Natural History of Cacao**. Washington, D.C.: Smithsonian Institution Press, 1994.

Articles

"Study: Chocolate Boost to Blood Vessel Health," **Associated Press**, Sunday, August 29, 2004.

Carnesecchi S, Schneider Y, Lazarus SA, et al. "Flavanols and Procyanidins of Cocoa and Chocolate Inhibit Growth of Polyamine Biosynthesis of Human Colonic Cancer Cells." **Cancer Lett**. 2002; 175:147-155.

Holt R.R., Lazarus S.A., Sullards M.C., et al. Procyanidin Dimer B2 (epicatechin-(4beta-8) — epicatechin) In Human Plasma After The Consumption of Flavanol-Rich Cocoa. Am J **Clin Nutr**. 2002; 76:1106-1110.

Kris-Etherton, P.M., Keen, C.L. "Evidence That The Antioxidant Flavonoids in Tea and Cocoa are Beneficial for Cardiovascular Health." **Curr Opin Lipidol**. 2002; 13:41-49.

Land, Ruth, "Loving Luxury Chocolate," **Money Magazine**, February 9, 2004

Olson, Elizabeth, "Beyond Delicious: Could Chocolate Also Be Good For You?," **New York Times**, February 17, 2004.

Osakabe, N, Baba S, Yasuda A, et al. "Daily Cocoa Intake Reduces The Susceptibility of Low-Density Lipoprotein To Oxidation As Demonstrated In Healthy Human Volunteers," **Free Rad Res**. 2001; 34:93-99.

Richelle, M, Tavazzi I, Offord E, "Comparison of the Antioxidant Activity of Commonly Consumed Polyphenolic Beverages (Coffee, Cocoa, Tea) Prepared Per Cup Serving," **J Agric Food Chem**. 2001;49:3438-3442.

Rios LY, Bennett RN, Lazarus SA, et al. "Cocoa Procyanidins Are Stable During Gastric Transit In Humans," **Am J Clin Nutr**. 2002; 76:1106-1110.

Schewe T, Kuhn H, Sies H, "Flavonoids of Cocoa Inhibit Recombinant Human 5-Lipoxygenase," **J Nutr**. 2002; 132: 1825-1829.

Web sites

groups.yahoo.com/group/nhnenews/message/5848

www.chocolate.org (regarding longevity)

www.news.cornell.edu/releases/Nov03/HotCocoa-Lee.bpf.html

news.bbc.co.uk/2/hi/health/3756997.stm (citing the **Journal of the American College of Nutrition** and the journal **Circulation**)

Methylxanthines: Theobromine and Caffeine

Books

Coe, Sophie D. and Coe, Michael D. **The True History of Chocolate**. New York: Thames and Hudson, 1996.

Kilham, Chris. **Psyche Delicacies: Coffee, Chocolate, Chiles, Kava, and Cannabis, and Why They're Good For You**. Emmaus, PA: Rodale Press, 2001.

Lopez, Ruth. **Chocolate: The Nature of Indulgence**. New York: Harry N. Abrams, 2002.

The Merck Index, 12th Edition

Pendell, Dale. **Pharmako/Dynamis: Stimulating Plants, Potions, and Herbcraft**. Revised edition. Berkeley, CA: North Atlantic Books, 2010.

Presilla, Maricel E. **The New Taste of Chocolate: A Cultural and Natural History of Cacao with Recipes**. Berkeley, CA: Ten Speed Press, 2001.

Young, Allen M. **The Chocolate Tree: A Natural History of Cacao**. Washington, D.C.: Smithsonian Institution Press, 1994.

Articles

The Biochemist, (Apr/May 1993, p 15) (Analyses of cacao demonstrating low caffeine content)

"The Republic of 'Gran Cacao'" (no author cited): **Slow Food Magazine**, April 2003, pgs 22-31.

Coe, Michael D. "In the Beginning was Kakaw." **Slow Food Magazine**, April 2003, pgs 40-43.

DeMartini, V., et al., "Theobromine as a Potential Cariostatic Agent," Friuli Med., 24: 525, 1969. (From **Chemical Abstracts** 75: 18302h, 1971).

Fries, J.H., "Chocolate, a Review of Published Reports of Allergic and Other Deleterious Effects, Real or Presumed," **Annals of Allergy**, 41: 195, 1978.

Fulton, J.E., et al., "Effect of Chocolate on Acne Vulgaris," **Journal of the American Medical Association**, 210: 2071, 1969.

Moffett, A.M. et al. "Effect of Chocolate in Migraine: A Double-Blind

Study," **Journal of Neurology, Neurosurgery and Psychiatry**, 37: 445, 1974.

Ott, Jonathan, **The Cacahuatl Eater: Ruminations Of An Unabashed Chocolate Addict**, Vashon, Washington, Natural Products Co., 1985.

Park, C.E., et al., "Inhibitory Effect of Cocoa Powder on the Growth of a Variety of Bacteria in Different Media," **Canadian Journal of Microbiology** 25: 233, 1979.

Stralfors, A., "Effect on Hamster Caries by Purine Derivatives, Vanillin and Some Tannin-Containing Materials," **Archives of Oral Biology**, 12: 321, 1967.

Vince, Gaia, "Persistent Coughs Melt Away with Chocolate,"**New Scientist**, (18:41), November 22, 2004. Citing: Federation of American Societies for Experimental Biology Journal (DOI: 10.1096/fj.04-1990fje)

Web sites
www.uspharmacist.com "The Health Benefits of Dark Chocolate," George Nemecz, PhD (Vol. No. 29:02, posted 2/15/4)

www.mrkland.com/fun/xocoatl/caffeine.htm

www.gourmed.gr/greekfood/show.asp?gid=9&nodeid=78&arid=3823

Phenylethylamine (PEA)

Books
Brenner, Joel Glenn. **The Emperors of Chocolate**, Broadway Books: New York, p. 96

Dahl, Roald. **Charlie and the Chocolate Factory**. New York: Puffin Books, copyright 1964, 1998 edition.

Drapeau, MSc., Christian. **Primordial Food (Aphanizomenon Flos-Aquae)**, One World Press, Asheville, North Carolina, 2003

Relevant Sites on page 58-59 (references 71 to 81) in **Primordial Food** by Christian Drapeau, MSc.

1. Sandler et al. (1979) Decreased cerebrospinal fluid concentration of free phenylacetic acid in depressive illness. **Clin Chim Acta** 93(1): 169-71.

2. Sabelli et al. (1983) Urinary phenyl acetate: a diagnostic test for depression? **Science** 220(4602): 1187-8.

3. Sabelli et al. (1996) Sustained antidepressant effect of PEA replacement. **J Neuropsychiatry Clin Neurosci** 8(2): 168-71.

4. Finberg et al. (2000) Modification of dopamine release by selective inhibitors of MAO-B. **Neurobiology** (Bp) 8(2):137-42.

5. Mosnaim et al. (1973) Ultraviolet spectrophotometric determination of 2-phenylethylamine in biological samples and its possible correlation with depression. **Biol Psychiatry** 6(3):235-57.

6. Mosnaim et al. (1974) The influence of psychotropic drugs on the levels of endogenous 2-phenylethylamine in rabbit brain. **Biol Psychiatry** 8(2):227-34.

7. Sabelli and Mosnaim (1974) Phenylethylamine hypothesis of affective behavior. **Am J Psychiat** 131:695-699.

8. Drapeau et al. (2002) Antidepressant properties of the blue-green algae **Aphanizomenon flos-aquae**. Annual meeting of the American Holistic Medicine Association, Toronto, May 2002.

9. Baker et al. (1991) Phenylethylaminergic mechanisms in attention-deficit disorder. **Biol Psychiatry** 29(1):15-22.

10. Parker and Cubeddu (1988) Comparative effects of amphetamine, phenylethylamine and related drugs on dopamine efflux, dopamine uptake and mazindol binding. **J Pharmacol Exp Ther** 245(1):199-210.

11. Sabelli and Javaid (1995) Phenylethylamine modulation of affect: thera-peutic and diagnostic implications. **J Neuropsychiatry Clin Neurosci** 7(1):6-14.

Kilham, Chris. **Psyche Delicacies: Coffee, Chocolate, Chiles, Kava, and Cannabis, and Why They're Good For You**. Emmaus, PA: Rodale Press, 2001.

Pendell, Dale. **Pharmako/Dynamis: Stimulating Plants, Potions, and Herbcraft**. Revised edition. Berkeley, CA: North Atlantic Books, 2010.

Articles

Simao, Paul, Study Links Marijuana Buzz, "Runner's High", **Reuters**, Atlanta, Jan. 9

Web sites

www.mrkland.com/fun/xocoatl/caffeine.htm

www.chocolate.org

Anandamide (The Bliss Chemical)

Books

Brenner, Joel Glenn. **The Emperors of Chocolate**, Broadway Books: New York, p. 96

Kilham, Chris. **Psyche Delicacies: Coffee, Chocolate, Chiles, Kava, and Cannabis, and Why They're Good For You**. Emmaus, PA: Rodale Press, 2001.

Pendell, Dale. **Pharmako/Dynamis: Stimulating Plants, Potions, and Herbcraft**. Revised edition. Berkeley, CA: North Atlantic Books, 2010.

Articles

Simao, Paul, Study Links Marijuana Buzz, "Runner's High", **Reuters**, Atlanta, Jan. 9

Web sites

www.chocolate.org

Neurotransmitter Modulating Agents

Books

Cousens, Gabriel, MD with Mark Mayell. **Depression-Free for Life.** New York: Harper Collins, 2001.

Tryptophan

Books

Cousens, Gabriel, M.D. with Mark Mayell. **Depression-Free for Life**. New York: Harper Collins, 2001.

References Part III: Exotic Properties of Chocolate

Aphrodisia

Books

Coe, Sophie D. and Coe, Michael D. **The True History of Chocolate**. New York: Thames and Hudson, 1996.

Kilham, Chris. **Psyche Delicacies: Coffee, Chocolate, Chiles, Kava, and Cannabis, and Why They're Good For You**. Emmaus, PA: Rodale Press, 2001.

Lopez, Ruth. **Chocolate: The Nature of Indulgence**. New York: Harry N. Abrams, 2002.

Morgenthaler, J. and Joy, D. **Better Sex Through Chemistry**. Petaluma, California: Smart Publications, 1995.

Pendell, Dale. **Pharmako/Dynamis: Stimulating Plants, Potions, and Herbcraft**. Revised edition. Berkeley, CA: North Atlantic Books, 2010.

Presilla, Maricel E. **The New Taste of Chocolate: A Cultural and Natural History of Cacao with Recipes**. Berkeley, CA: Ten Speed Press, 2001.

Nobility

Books

Coe, Sophie D. and Coe, Michael D. **The True History of Chocolate**. New York: Thames and Hudson, 1996.

Pendell, Dale. **Pharmako/Dynamis: Stimulating Plants, Potions, and Herbcraft**. Revised edition. Berkeley, CA: North Atlantic Books, 2010.

Nature's Prozac (Anti-Depressant Properties of Cacao)

Books

Cousens, Gabriel, M.D. with Mark Mayell. **Depression-Free for Life**. New York: Harper Collins, 2001.

Dahl, Roald. **Charlie and the Chocolate Factory**. New York: Puffin Books, copyright 1964, 1998 edition.

Kilham, Chris. **Psyche Delicacies: Coffee, Chocolate, Chiles, Kava, and Cannabis, and Why They're Good For You**. Emmaus, PA: Rodale Press, 2001.

Pendell, Dale. **Pharmako/Dynamis: Stimulating Plants, Potions, and Herbcraft**. Revised edition. Berkeley, CA: North Atlantic Books, 2010.

Tryptamines, Phenylalanines, Lactones and Cannabinoids

Books

Coe, Sophie D. and Coe, Michael D. **The True History of Chocolate**. New York: Thames and Hudson, 1996.

Kilham, Chris. **Psyche Delicacies: Coffee, Chocolate, Chiles, Kava, and Cannabis, and Why They're Good For You**. Emmaus, PA: Rodale Press, 2001.

Lopez, Ruth. **Chocolate: The Nature of Indulgence**, New York: Harry N. Abrams, 2002.

Ott, Jonathon. **Pharmacotheon** (2nd Edition densified). Kennewick, Washington, Natural Products Co., 1996.

Pendell, Dale. **Pharmako/Dynamis: Stimulating Plants, Potions, and Herbcraft**. Revised edition. Berkeley, CA: North Atlantic Books, 2010.

Presilla, Maricel E. **The New Taste of Chocolate: A Cultural and Natural History of Cacao with Recipes**. Berkeley, CA: Ten Speed Press, 2001.

Young, Allen M. **The Chocolate Tree: A Natural History of Cacao**. Washington, D.C.: Smithsonian Institution Press, 1994.

Articles

"Food of the Gods: Cure for Humanity? A Cultural History of the Medicinal and Ritual Use of Chocolate" by Dillinger T.L., Barriga P., Escarcega S., Jimenez M., Salazar Lowe D., Grivetti L.E., Department of Nutrition, University of California, Davis CA 95616, USA., J Nutr 2000 Aug; 130(8S Suppl):2057S-72S

"The Republic of 'Gran Cacao'" (no author cited): **Slow Food Magazine**, April 2003, pgs 22-31.

Coe, Michael D. "In the Beginning was Kakaw." **Slow Food Magazine**, April 2003, pgs 40-43.

Herraiz T., "Tetrahydro-beta-carbolines, potential neuroactive alkaloids, in chocolate and cocoa." **J Agric Food Chem**, 2000;48:4900–4904

Raffauf, R.F., and Zennie, T.M. "The Phytochemistry of Quararibea Funebris." **Botanical Museum Leaflets**, Harvard University. 29(2): 151-157 (1983).

Web sites

www.chocolate.org

www.erowid.com

www.thc4ms.org.uk

Chocolate As Medicine

Books

Coe, Sophie D. and Coe, Michael D. **The True History of Chocolate**. New York: Thames and Hudson, 1996.

Dahl, Roald. **Charlie and the Chocolate Factory**. New York: Puffin Books, copyright 1964, 1998 edition.

Foster, Nelson and Cordell, Linda S. **Chilies to Chocolate: Food the Americas Gave the World**. Tucson, AZ: University of AZ Press, 1992.

Kilham, Chris. **Psyche Delicacies: Coffee, Chocolate, Chiles, Kava, and Cannabis, and Why They're Good For You**. Emmaus, PA: Rodale Press, 2001.

Lopez, Ruth. **Chocolate: The Nature of Indulgence**. New York: Harry N. Abrams, 2002.

McFadden, Christine and France, Christine. **Chocolate: Cooking with the World's Best Ingredient**. London: Hermes House, 1997.

Ott, Jonathan. **The Cacahuatl Eater: Ruminations Of An Unabashed Chocolate Addict**, Vashon, Washington, Natural Products Co., 1985.

Pendell, Dale. **Pharmako/Dynamis: Stimulating Plants, Potions, and Herbcraft**. Revised edition. Berkeley, CA: North Atlantic Books, 2010.

Presilla, Maricel E. **The New Taste of Chocolate: A Cultural and Natural History of Cacao with Recipes**. Berkeley, CA: Ten Speed Press, 2001.

Young, Allen M. **The Chocolate Tree: A Natural History of Cacao**. Washington, D.C.: Smithsonian Institution Press, 1994.

Articles

"The Republic of 'Gran Cacao'" (no author cited): **Slow Food Magazine**, April 2003, pgs 22-31.

Coe, Michael D. "In the Beginning was Kakaw." **Slow Food Magazine**, April 2003, pgs 40-43.

Web sites

Daily Telegraph, UK, Section: Magazine, Saturday, February 22 2003, Author: David Rowan, Web: www.telegraph.co.uk, Cited: Legalise Cannabis Alliance www.lca-uk.org, THC4MS www.thc4ms.org.uk

Chocolate and Pregnancy

Articles

"Chocolate During Pregnancy Has Good Impact on Baby", **Reuters**, London, Tuesday, April 6, 2004

Christian M.S., Brent, R.L. "Teratogen Update: Evaluation of the Reproductive and Developmental Risks of Caffeine." **Teratology**. 2001;64:51-78.

Chocolate Yoga

No relevant citations.

Overcoming Chocolate Addictions

Articles

"Chocolate: Food or Drug?" by Bruinsma K, Taren DL

Arizona Prevention Center, University of Arizona, College of Medicine, Tucson 85719, USA, J Am Diet Assoc, 1999 Oct; 99(10):1249-56

Web sites

www.nwu.edu

"Measuring Brain Activity In People Eating Chocolate Offers New Clues About How The Body Becomes Addicted" (Source: Northwestern University, Date: Posted 8/29/2001)

www.chocolate.org

Saving The Planet With Chocolate

Books

Coe, Sophie D. and Coe, Michael D. **The True History of Chocolate**. New York: Thames and Hudson, 1996.

Foster, Nelson and Cordell, Linda S. **Chilies to Chocolate: Food the Americas Gave the World**. Tucson, AZ: University of AZ Press, 1992.

Kilham, Chris. **Psyche Delicacies: Coffee, Chocolate, Chiles, Kava, and Cannabis, and Why They're Good For You**. Emmaus, PA: Rodale Press, 2001.

Lopez, Ruth. **Chocolate: The Nature of Indulgence**. New York: Harry N. Abrams, 2002.

Pendell, Dale. **Pharmako/Dynamis: Stimulating Plants, Potions, and Herbcraft**. Revised edition. Berkeley, CA: North Atlantic Books, 2010.

Presilla, Maricel E. **The New Taste of Chocolate: A Cultural and Natural History of Cacao with Recipes**. Berkeley, CA: Ten Speed Press, 2001.

Young, Allen M. **The Chocolate Tree: A Natural History of Cacao**. Washington, D.C.: Smithsonian Institution Press, 1994.

Articles

Bertotto, Marco, "Child Slaves," **Slow Food Magazine**, April 2003.

Rice, Robert A., Greenberg, Russell, "The Chocolate Tree," **Natural History**, July, 2003 p. 36-43

Web sites

www.progress.org/gandhi/gandhi02.htm

www.ivu.org/history/gandhi/experiments.html

www.pan-uk.org/banlindane/lindchoc.htm (News Release: 12/04/2001)

References Part IV, Chocolate Alchemy

Books

Coe, Sophie D. and Coe, Michael D. **The True History of Chocolate**. New York: Thames and Hudson, 1996.

Dahl, Roald. **Charlie and the Chocolate Factory**. New York: Puffin Books, copyright 1964, 1998 edition.

Foster, Nelson and Cordell, Linda S. **Chilies to Chocolate: Food the Americas Gave the World**. Tucson, AZ: University of AZ Press, 1992.

Kilham, Chris. **Psyche Delicacies: Coffee, Chocolate, Chiles, Kava, and Cannabis, and Why They're Good For You**. Emmaus, PA: Rodale Press, 2001.

Lopez, Ruth. **Chocolate: The Nature of Indulgence**. New York: Harry N. Abrams, 2002.

McFadden, Christine and France, Christine. **Chocolate: Cooking with the World's Best Ingredient**. London: Hermes House, 1997.

Ott, Jonathan. **The Cacahuatl Eater: Ruminations Of An Unabashed Chocolate Addict**, Vashon, Washington, Natural Products Co., 1985.

Pendell, Dale. **Pharmako/Dynamis: Stimulating Plants, Potions, and Herbcraft**. Revised edition. Berkeley, CA: North Atlantic Books, 2010.

Presilla, Maricel E. **The New Taste of Chocolate: A Cultural and Natural History of Cacao with Recipes**. Berkeley, CA: Ten Speed Press, 2001.

Young, Allen M., **The Chocolate Tree: A Natural History of Cacao**. Washington, D.C.: Smithsonian Institution Press, 1994.

Articles

"The Republic of 'Gran Cacao'" (no author cited): **Slow Food Magazine**, April 2003, pgs 22-31.

Coe, Michael D. "In the Beginning was Kakaw." **Slow Food Magazine**, April 2003, pgs 40-43.

Photo Credits

Aarona Pichinson (www.yogaofnourishment.com)
Anita Arze (www.anitaarze.com)
Bob Arnott (www.bobarnott.com)
Danielle Carney
David Wolfe (www.davidwolfe.com)
Matt Barratt
Shazzie (www.shazzie.com)
Zak Shuman (zakoptic@hotmail.com)

Other Books & Projects by Shazzie

Books and Ebooks

Detox Delights — An all-time detox classic, now in its fifth edition. Over 100 simple and delicious recipes to help you feel great all over.

Detox Your World — nearly 400 pages of life-changing information. Includes 100 new detox recipes and five detox plans.

Evie's Kitchen — The world's first comprehensive guide to raising a child with living foods. Contains full colour superfood recipes and natural parenting information.

Ecstatic Beings — Co-authored with Kate Magic, this huge mega coloured coffee table book on living life ecstatically became an instant cult classic.

Raw Britannia — A free ebook to help you start on raw foods.

Shazzie Whispers — Free transformation training guide.

Shazzie Speaks — A program to detox your mind.

Divinity in a Box — A program to help you find your magic dharma key. Discover your real essence and path with this virtual workshop.

Shazzie's VIP Room — The place that helps you reveal the divine being lurking within. Thousands of life mastery tools and tips.

DVD

Shazzie's Delights — a set of three raw food preparation DVDs, for breakfast, lunch and dinner.

Web sites

shazzie.com

shazziesVIProom.com

detoxyourworld.com (massive online shop)

rawcreation.com

shazziespeaks.com

divinityinabox.com

facebook.com/shazzieFB

twitter.com/doxtor

youtube.com/valerie1969

Chocolate Resources in the UK and Europe!

www.detoxyourworld.com

Yes! You can find all those unusual products that are mentioned in this book (as well as more copies of this book) and so much more right here:

- Shazzie's Naked Chocolate, raw organic chocolate bars
- Cacao beans, nibs, liquor, butter, powder
- Goji berries, Incan berries
- Maca powder
- Agave cactus nectar
- Spirulina, dried wheatgrass, green superfoods
- Carob powder
- Coconut oil
- Dehydrators
- Vita-Mix/VitaPrep
- Ionisers

- Distillers
- Eco yoga mats
- InnerTalk CDs
- Safe toiletries
- Teas
- Herbs
- Books, Videos and DVDs
- Juicers
- Supplements such as ionic minerals
- Magnotherapy
- SAD lightboxes
- Exercise equipment

Over 700 other wonderful reasons to visit us!

08700 113 119

(int: +44 8700 113 119)
Established 2000

sales@detoxyourworld.com

Shop:
www.detoxyourworld.com

detoxyourworld.wordpress.com

facebook.com/detoxyourworld

twitter.com/detoxyourworld

youtube.com/detoxyourworld

DETOXYOURWORLD

Other Books & Projects by David Wolfe

Books, DVDs and Programs

The Sunfood Diet Success System
Eating for Beauty
Superfoods: The Food and Medicine of the Future
Naked Chocolate
The LongevityNOW Program
Superfood Recipes (DVD)
Superherb Recipes (DVD)
Chaga: King of the Medicinal Mushrooms

Web sites

www.davidwolfe.com

www.sacredchocolate.com

www.thebestdayever.com

www.longevitywarehouse.com

www.rawnutritioncertification.com

www.thelongevitynowconference.com

www.ftpf.org

www.facebook.com/DavidAvocadoWolfe

www.twitter.com/DavidWolfe

www.youtube.com/DavidAvocadoWolfe

Sacred Chocolate

www.sacredchocolate.com

"Sacred Chocolate™ is clearly the best chocolate bar ever. Take one bite and you will know that Sacred Chocolate™ has cracked the cacao code!"

—David Wolfe

Sacred Chocolate™ is committed to bringing you the highest quality chocolate ever. From the cacao bean to each chocolate bar, Sacred Chocolate™ is infused with love, prayer, and gratitude. We honor, respect, and give thanks to all beings that make the amazing superfood known as chocolate possible. To our Sacred Chocolate™ team, this food is a holy sacrament, an offering to the higher power, and a superfood for positive life transformation.

Our special, organic, dark, raw chocolate products are made over several weeks, the old-fashioned way: we slowly stone-grind our raw cacao beans at a low temperature. Our beans are never roasted, and all processes are kept below 114 degrees Fahrenheit to ensure maximum antioxidant retention and zero trans-fatty acid production. Sacred Chocolate™ has an antioxidant rating (ORAC score) three to four times higher than that of a cooked dark chocolate bar of comparable cacao content.

Sacred Chocolate™ is the only chocolate product in the world that (whenever available) includes the microbe-free skin of the cacao bean for flavor and nutritional purposes. The delicate skin adds a fruity complexity to the flavor of Sacred Chocolate™ and also adds concentrated phytonutrients, analogous to the nutrition found in the skin of most fruits and vegetables. Sacred Chocolate™ uses certifiably vegan, organic maple sugar in all sweetened recipes. The maple bouquet adds a rich complexity to the fruity aromica bean. Also, by using maple, old-growth forests thrive—trees are not cut down to produce it. Maple rates low with a score of fifty-five on the glycemic index, and contains manganese, zinc, and potassium, as well as antioxidants including epicatechins and quercetin.

Sacred Chocolate™ donates to the Fruit Tree Planting Foundation (ftpf.org).

www.sacredchocolate.com

"Open the Heart . . . Discover the Magic!"

David Wolfe's Online Magazine

www.thebestdayever.com

A Special Message from David Wolfe: I have so many tapes of my past lectures, so many notes I have taken over the years, so many great health and success secrets, so many incredible bits of information that my office and I are overloaded. I literally spent a couple years wondering what to do with all this great stuff! Should I put it into more books? More DVDs? More audio recordings? This stuff is not doing the planet any good sitting here in my office! Then I met an individual who recommended that I start a subscription website. I did! Now all this material is on-line at thebestdayever.com! This new regularly updated website gives you complete ACCESS to my audio and text library containing dozens of lectures and CONFIDENTIAL files on chocolate, nutrition, health, minerals, rejuvenation programs and exotic information. If you are inspired to achieve an exceptional state of health, success, beauty, fitness, awareness, joy, sensuality, accomplishment, peak performance and most importantly fun, then thebestdayever.com is for you!

The Fruit Tree Planting Foundation

www.ftpf.org | info@ftpf.org

The Fruit Tree Planting Foundation is a 501(c)3 non-profit organization founded by David Wolfe

The goal of The Fruit Tree Planting Foundation is to plant 18 billion heirloom fruit trees, encouraging their growth under organic standards and creating settings of rich ecological, sustainable and life-enhancing diversity.

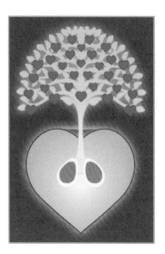

It has been estimated that 18 billion trees need to be planted in order to reverse the damage done to the atmosphere. The Foundation decided that as long as we were going to participate in planting trees to save the environment, we should plant edible fruit trees, such as cacao!

Your 501(c)3 tax-deductible charitable investment will help us realize our dream of a sustainable planet for generations to come. As you find you are interested in donating, please visit our website and donate online:

The Fruit Tree Planting Foundation
www.ftpf.org

While we will be sending you a receipt for your donation, you may want to make a note of this transaction for tax purposes. Thank you for taking action on this important issue.

About The Authors

David Wolfe (a.k.a. Chocolate Pope Avocado Noni Cacao): Considered by peers to be one of the world's leading nutrition authorities, David Wolfe is the author of **Superfoods: The Food and Medicine of the Future, Eating For Beauty**, **The Sunfood Diet Success System** as well as **The LongevityNOW Program**.

Over the last 18 years, as a health and personal success speaker, David has hosted over 2,500 inspirational lectures, seminars and dinners along with dozens of adventure retreats all over the world. At these events he inspires people to optimize their health and achieve their full potential by employing positive thinking, superior nutrition and, of course, by eating chocolate!

David has appeared on hundreds of broadcast programs and in print media around the world. David has consulted and inspired numerous start-up raw and established chocolate companies including the ever-popular Sacred Chocolate (www.sacredchocolate.com).

Shazzie: Born in East Yorkshire, UK, in 1969, Shazzie had a typical northern lifestyle and diet in her formative years. As an adult,

she suffered lethargy, depression, brain-fog, bad skin and aches and pains — until she created a detox and rejuvenation programme for herself. These days she feels younger than ever before, has relentless energy and a body which functions as it should! Shazzie spreads the secrets that she's uncovered to millions of people throughout the world via her web sites, books, magazine columns, workshops and retreats.

Shazzie is mummy to Evie, born on 5th August 2004. She is now doubly committed to making the world a more beautiful place for the sake of all the babies on this planet.

Naked Chocolate is Shazzie's third book, and it follows in the footsteps of the hugely popular **Detox Your World** and **Detox Delights**.

"The superiority of chocolate for health and nourishment will soon give it the same preference over tea and coffee in America that it has in Spain."

— Thomas Jefferson